# USA Investment Visa to Green Card

How to Qualify, Apply and Obtain
EB-5, E-2, L-1 Visa

**Complete A to Z Guide**

**BY**

Shabbir Hossain

Karen McCarthy

*Copyright © 2016 - CSB Academy Publishing Company*

All Rights Reserved.
*No part of this publication may be reproduced, stored in a retrieval system or transmitted in any form or by any means, electronic, mechanical, photocopying, recording or otherwise without the proper written consent of the copyright holder, except brief quotations used in a review.*

Published by:

**CSB Academy Publishing Company.**
P.O. Box 966
Semmes, Alabama 36575

Cover & Interior designed
By

David Miller

*First Edition*

## Table Of Contents

Foreword .................................................................................9
What is An Investment Visa? ................................................13
   Type Of Investment Visas ..................................................13
      EB-5 Investment Visa ....................................................13
      E-2 Investment Visa ......................................................14
      L-1 Visa ........................................................................15
International Immigrant Investor Programs .........................17
   Australia .............................................................................17
   Belgium .............................................................................18
   Bulgaria .............................................................................19
   Canada ..............................................................................20
   Dominican Republic ..........................................................20
   France ...............................................................................21
   Germany ............................................................................22
   Japan .................................................................................23
   Netherlands .......................................................................23
   New Zealand .....................................................................24
   Portugal .............................................................................24
   South Korea ......................................................................25
   Spain ..................................................................................25
   Switzerland ........................................................................26
   United Kingdom ................................................................27
United States and Birth of EB-5 Visa ...................................28
   EB-5 Program History .......................................................28
3 Main Requirements of EB-5 Visa ......................................32
   Business Entity Requirements ..........................................32
   Job Creation Requirements ..............................................33
   Capital Investment Requirements ....................................35

5 Steps to Getting an EB-5 Visa ................................................. 37
Step-1: Choosing an EB-5 Project ............................................. 38
   Direct Investment vs. Regional Center Investment ......... 38
   The Basics of Direct Investment ............................................. 38
      What is an EB-5 Business? .............................................. 39
      Types of EB-5 Businesses ............................................... 40
      Tips for Choosing an EB-5 Business .............................. 40
   Regional Center Investment ................................................... 42
   What is an EB-5 Regional Center? ......................................... 43
      Forming a Regional Center .............................................. 44
   How to Use a Regional Center for Investment ................... 45
      1, Identify the Regional Center ........................................ 47
      2. Due Diligence ................................................................ 48
      3. Approvals of Forms I-526 / I-829 ................................ 48
      4. Compliance ..................................................................... 49
      5. Negotiate Terms ............................................................ 49
      6. Contract ........................................................................... 50
   Why Become a Regional Center? ........................................... 51
   How to Become a Regional Center ....................................... 52
   Steps to Become an EB-5 Regional Center ......................... 53
      Determine the Scope ........................................................ 54
      Hire Professional Services for Regional Center Filing 54
      Business Plan Writer ......................................................... 55
      Economist ........................................................................... 56
      Securities Counsel ............................................................. 57
      I-924 Petition ..................................................................... 58
      I-924 Requirements .......................................................... 58
      Filing I-924 ......................................................................... 60
      I-526 Petitions ................................................................... 61

Form I-526 .................................................................. 61
I-526 Requirements ................................................... 63
Filing the I-526 .......................................................... 64
I-829 Petitions by EB-5 Visa Applicants ..................... 65
Advantages of a Regional Center Investment ............... 66
Regional Center Statistics ......................................... 68
Step -2: Meet Job Creation Requirements ...................... 69
Job Requirements for Regional Centers and Direct Investments ................................................................ 70
Direct Jobs ............................................................. 71
Indirect Jobs ........................................................... 71
Induced Jobs .......................................................... 72
Qualified Employee ................................................... 72
Troubled Businesses ................................................. 73
Targeted Employment Area ....................................... 73
What is a Rural Area? .............................................. 74
What is a High Unemployment Area? ....................... 74
How to Get TEA Designation ................................... 75
Step-3: EB-5 Project Investment Capital and I-526 Petition ................................................................................ 77
What is EB-5 Capital? .............................................. 77
Back Story of the EB-5 Program .............................. 78
Regional Center Designation ................................... 79
Affiliate with an Existing Regional Center ................. 80
Direct Investment ..................................................... 80
Choosing an Investment Method ............................ 81
What to Keep in Mind ............................................... 83
Step-4: Two Year Conditional Permanent Residency ........ 84
An I-485 Application ................................................. 85

- Components of the I-485 Application ..........86
- Filing the I-485 ..........87
  - What is DS-230 Application ..........89
- Step-5: Unconditional Permanent Residency and I-829 Petition ..........91
  - I-829 Petition ..........91
  - I-829 Requirements ..........92
  - Filing the I-829 ..........94
  - EB-5 Service Providers ..........95
    - Legal Counsel ..........95
    - Business Plan Preparation ..........96
    - Economists ..........99
    - Marketing Company ..........100
    - Due Diligence ..........101
  - What to Ask a Regional Center ..........101
    - Investor Profile and EB-5 Involvement ..........102
  - Timing ..........103
  - Job Creation ..........104
  - Due Diligence ..........104
    - Has the Regional Center Actually Been Designated by USCIS? ..........105
    - What is the Regional Center's Track Record? ..........105
    - How Long the Regional Center Been Operational and How Many Projects Has It Sponsored ..........106
    - What is the Reputation of the Project Developer? ..........107
    - What is the Reputation and Experience of the Project Developer's outside Counsel and Consultants? ..........107
    - Has the Project Been Pre-Approved by the USCIS? ..........107
    - Is the Project Being Developed in a Targeted Employment Area (TEA)? ..........108

How Will the EB-5 Funds Be Released to the Project? ...... 108

How Are Funds Returned to the Investor If I-526 Petition is Denied? ...... 108

What is the Exit Strategy? ...... 109

What is the Rate of Return? ...... 109

Is There a Job Cushion? ...... 109

When Will Job Creation Occur? ...... 110

What Type of Investment Is Being Made with the Investor's Funds and How Are Jobs Created? ...... 110

What Percentage of the Total Capital Stack is Comprised of EB-5 Money? ...... 110

How Credible is the Business Plan? ...... 111

Permanent Residency ...... 111

E-2 Visa A to Z Explained ...... 113

E-2 Investor Visa Qualification Requirements ...... 113

Additional E-2 Investor Visa-Related Information ...... 115

Benefits of E-2 Visa ...... 115

10 Most Commonly Asked Questions About E-2 Visa . 116

Does the business need to be fully operational at the time of filing? ...... 116

What and How Much should I invest? ...... 117

What is considered a "substantial" investment? ...... 117

What is a "substantiality" test? ...... 118

Can I have part of the total business price financed by the seller? ...... 118

Does my investment need to be from Personal source? .... 119

Does the business need to create jobs? ...... 119

What is a "marginal" investment? ...... 120

What is an "essential" role in the business? ...... 120

Who can have the "essential roles"? ..........................121
List of Countries that have the Treaty for E-2 Visa ........121
   Countries that Maintain Treaties of Navigation and Commerce with the United States for E2 Visa Purposes ..........................................................................121
How to Apply For an E-2 Visa ............................................122
List of Documents you need to Apply .................................123
L-1 Visa A to Z Explained ........................................................125
  L-1 Visa requirements ........................................................126
  Benefits of L-1 Visa ............................................................126
  Types of L-1 Visa ................................................................126
    L-1A Visa Requirements .................................................127
    L-1B Visa requirements .................................................128
  Documents Required For L-1 Visa Application ...............129
    From the U.S. Company .................................................129
    From The Foreign Company ..........................................129
    From the Actual Applicant ...............................................130
  How to Convert L-1 Visa to Green Card ..........................130
Which Visa is More Suitable For Small Retail Business Like a Gas Station Business ...........................................................132
  7 Most Popular businesses to Invest In ...........................132
Do These Visas Help You to Get Permanent Residency in The U.S.? ................................................................................134
  7 Safety Measures to Protect your Investment ...............136
  Rights of Permanent Residents ........................................137
  Responsibilities of Permanent Residents ........................137
  Permanent Residency vs. Citizenship .............................138
Resources ...............................................................................140

# Foreword

As an immigrant myself I have always been fascinated by various types of visas and immigration opportunities that countries like the U.S. and other western nations offer to different foreign nationals. People migrate to other nations for various reasons but looking back I can tell you the top four reasons most people I know migrate to countries like the USA, Great Britain, and other western countries:
1. Education
2. Financial future
3. Safety and security
4. Freedom

There are many immigration programs most all western countries offer to other foreign nationals simply because these Western countries want to create more diversity, increase innovation and to bring foreign investment.
The U.S. has been the most successful country in the world in terms of education, safety, financial future and freedom for more than a century. One of the main contributing factors for its success has been its immigration policy. For centuries people from all around the world came and settled in the USA and made it one of the most diversified countries. The goal for the U.S immigration and the lawmakers have always been to attract the best and the brightest people from all walks of life and culture, so the

country can prosper from the contribution of all the talents. Diversity in a population is always a strength and never a weakness, the countries that understood that early on are the ones that became very successful.

I am not an immigration attorney or an immigration adviser, I am not qualified to advise anyone on this topic, but what I am is a business coach, a consultant, and a small business owner. I started a blog, http://gasstationbusiness101.com a few years ago to teach aspiring entrepreneurs how to start, run and grow a gas station business successfully. Around the same time, I wrote a book also on this very topic. Since then every week I receive few emails from people asking various small business questions, but have never had anyone ask me about immigration or investment visa questions.

Beginning of this year, I received a heartfelt email from a gentleman asking me for advice as he was in the process of buying a gas station in Chicago. But unfortunately, he was dealing with some dishonest business broker along with a dishonest seller both of whom were trying to take his money and not sell him any business. Long story short, in distress, he found my podcast show and emailed me for advice.

I had to do some serious research on E-2 visa, as that was the category he was applying for, and eventually gave him some advice and asked him to hire an attorney to handle the transaction. Thankfully he was able to avoid the disaster with help from a good attorney.

After that initial research I got interested in this vast topic of investment visas, and started doing more research. During the process, I met Karen who worked as the legal assistant for an immigration attorney in Atlanta for almost 20 years.

Long story short, We both decided that we should combine my research and her expertise in a book for those that are looking for solid advice and clear understanding as to what the investment visas are, how to qualify for them, how to apply for them and how to get them approved.

We also included a chapter where we picked out the top 15 countries that have similar investment visa programs to what we have in the U.S. In that chapter you will find information on all the requirements on applying for an investment visa in countries like England, France, Australia, Canada, Belgium, Bulgaria, Germany and few more.

One word of advice for our readers; before investing any money with any business abroad with the intent of obtaining any visa, please ask for professional guidance from a qualified immigration attorney, it will save you money and heartache in the long run.

# What is An Investment Visa?

An investment visa is one type of immigration visa that foreign investors can get when they want to immigrate to the United States. There are different types of immigrant investor programs depending on the country you are in, but their main focus is to encourage foreign investment in exchange for either a conditional or permanent residency. Each country differs in its requirements for an investment visa as well in the types of investment visas offered. Each visa has its own amount of investment and awards a different type of residency. We'll look briefly at these later, but for now I want to discuss the two main types of investment visas offered in the United States - the EB-5 andE-2. Then there is L-1 visa which is not an investment visa but rather a intracompany transfer visa. But we will cover that visa in detail as well.

Type Of Investment Visas

EB-5 Investment Visa

The EB-5 investment visa is different from other visas available in the United States, including visas based on employment, the Diversity Immigrant Visa and family based visas. The EB-5 visa is the only employment based visa in the United States that requires investment.

The EB-5 visa provides foreign nationals with a way to get a green card and eventually citizenship in the United States. The Immigrant Investor (EB-5) Program is overseen by the United States Citizenship and Immigration Services. It offers an investment visa to any foreign investors who invest over $1 million into a new commercial enterprise in the United States or a $500,000 investment into a targeted employment area. In addition to the amount, the investment also needs to create at least 10 full-time jobs for United States workers. After these two criteria are met the foreign investor can then apply for a U.S. green card and eventually obtain permanent residence in the United States if the jobs are proven to have been created.

E-2 Investment Visa

In the United States, another type of investment visa is the E-2 Treaty Investors Visa. This is a non-immigrant that is available to foreign investors form a country that maintains a treaty of navigation and commerce with the United States. The applicant needs to invest capital in a business in the United States in order to receive the visa. With the E-2 Visa, specific employees of the investor or their authorized organization can also apply for the E-2 Visa. There is also an application process for investors' family members who want to get a U.S. Visa under the E-2 option.

Investors need to have already invested or begun the investment process for a substantial amount of funds into a genuine U.S. business in order to be approved for an E-2 Visa. Unlike the EB-5 Visa, the E-2 Visa does require renewal. However, the visa can be renewed an unlimited number of times. After the business venture is complete, the foreign investors either need to leave the United States or change their status since the E-2 doesn't directly lead to a green card and citizenship like the EB-5 Visa. But there are ways to E-2 visa holders can apply and get permanent residency and ultimately U.S. citizenship but it is not as simple as the EB-5 process. For this reason I want to focus mostly on the EB-5 Visa. But before we go into that, let's take a brief look at immigrant investor programs in other countries to see why the EB-5 Visa in the United States is a good option.

### L-1 Visa

L1 visa is a non-immigrant visa which allows companies operating both in the US and abroad to transfer certain classes of employee from its foreign operations to the USA operations for up to seven years. The employee must have worked for a subsidiary, parent, affiliate or branch office of your US company outside of the US for at least one year out of the last three years.

Normally nonimmigrant visa applicants are presumed to an immigrant and should provide satisfactory proof that they no intention of immigrating to the U.S. before obtaining the visa. However, the L type visa is a "dual intent" visa which means they are not required to maintain a foreign residence. Many L-1 visa holders can eventually apply for green cards and become permanent resident and eventually U.S. citizen over time. I will discuss more on this in a later chapter.

# International Immigrant Investor Programs

Many countries offer programs that allow foreign investors to gain residency similar to the EB-5 investment visa program in the United States. Most of these programs try to increase a country's foreign direct investment levels by providing the incentive of citizenship to those who make large investments. Each country differs in the requirements and residency status for their immigrant investment programs. For example, in some countries foreign investors gain full permanent residency as a part of the visa programs while others only offer a conditional residency. Let's take a look at some of them.

### Australia

The investment visa category in Australia offers foreign investors the chance to immigrate. However, unlike the EB-5 program that offers permanent residency, the Australian visa only allow foreign investors four years of temporary residency. After four years, the foreign investor must apply for other visa types in order to get permanent residency. The requirements for this visa are the following:
- Make an $1.5 million AUD investment in an Australian company in which the investor has an ownership stake
- The investors must be younger than 45
- The investors must have net assets of at least $2.25

million AUD
- They must have a vocational level of English language proficiency
- They must have business management experience of at least three years
- They must maintain a positive business record

## Belgium

Belgium is a popular location for investors seeking residency because of its highly developed infrastructure complete with airports, seaports, roadways, railways and numerous tax incentives. If qualifications are met, a residency permit will normally be granted within two to three months of getting a work permit. In the first three years, an annual renewal is required; but in the fourth year a permanent residence permit can be issued. After the residence permit is issued, a family reunion procedure allows an applicant's spouse and children to join the applicant as residents. The qualifications for this program include the following:

- There must be a proven personal, business or professional tie to Belgium. This can be done by setting up a company, investing in an existing Belgian company or working for a Belgian company.
- The applicant must be highly skilled or key personnel in a business.

- The company's share capital must be at least € 18,600, but being a shareholder of the company isn't required.
- A yearly salary of at least € 37,712 for a highly skilled employee or € 62,934 for an employee in a managerial position. There is no minimum salary requirement for individuals who are self-employed.

## Bulgaria

Bulgaria offers two options for foreign investors: a full investment or a financed investment. The loan period for each is five years. Applicants must have a clear criminal record in their birth country and country of residence in additional to the following qualifications:

For a full investment:
- A net worth greater than 1,000,000 BGN.
- Invest a minimum of 1,000,000 BGN in a fully guaranteed governmental bond portfolio for five years. At the end of the five years, the full amount will be returned to the investor without accrued interest.

For a financed investment:
- A net worth greater than 2,000,000 BGN.
- A deposit of € 180,000 is used to cover the costs of obtaining a loan from a chartered Bulgarian bank. The deposit is not returned to the investors.

## Canada

In Canada, the Federal Immigrant Investor Program offers foreign investors a way to gain Canadian residency. Unlike other countries, those who complete this program receive permanent residency status. Because of this there is a 700 applicant cap on the program and the backlog of applications has lead to an approximate 12 year wait for any new applications. The qualifications for this program are:

- A minimum net worth of $1.6 million CAD.
- At least two years of managerial experience.
- A five year investment of $800,000 CAD. The investment is managed by the Citizenship and Immigration Canada (CIC) and used to help with economic growth in Canadian provinces. The full amount is returned to the investor without interest after a five year and three month payment.

## Dominican Republic

When it comes to the Dominican Republic, foreign investors again have two options: they can choose to apply as a single applicant or as a family. For a single applicant, a non-refundable cash investment of $100,000 US is required. For a family applicant, the amount is either $175,000 US, $200,000 US or $350,000 US depending on the number of children. The process for these applications can take between six and fourteen months and include a personal review. In addition, the qualifications are:

- At least 21 years of age.
- Be of outstand character.
- No criminal record and a clean source of funds.
- A basic knowledge of the English language.
- A letter of intent addressed to the Minister for Citizenship.
- A government approved promoter/agent.

## France

The French Residence Permit Program allows foreign investors to live in France for ten years. There are no requirements surrounding prior residency, French residency, and profession or language skills. However, foreign investors are required to have no criminal convictions and be in good standing in regards to their residency rights on French territory. Investors need to make a long-term and non-speculative investment of € 10 million in either commercial or industrial assets in France. The investment can be through a company in which the investor owns at least 30 percent of the capital or it can be a personal investment.

# Germany

The German Investor Visa Program offers a way for foreign investors to get a residency permit. The investment requirements are the same for self-employed entrepreneurs. After having a residency permit for at least five years and sufficient knowledge of the German language, social and legal system, the applicant can then apply for permanent resident status. Foreign investors from the United States, Australia, New Zealand, Canada, Switzerland, Israel and Japan can apply for permanent residency while remaining a visitor. Foreign investors from other countries need to apply for and obtain a residency permit before entering Germany. The qualifications for this program include:

- The financial means and capability to invest € 1 million into a German project.
- Create a minimum of 10 new German job opportunities.
- A valid passport, relevant birth and marriage certificates and relevant documents detailing intent to reside in the country.
- A medical and health insurance policy that covers the individual to a value of € 30,000.
- Documentation proving sufficient means to support themselves and their family while living in Germany.

## Japan

The Japanese Investor Visa lasts for one or three years and has only two major requirements. First, an investor needs to have a minimum of three years experience in business management. Second, a minimum investment of 5 million yen in a Japanese business or already have a business in Japan that employs at least two full-time legal residents. The investment doesn't need to establish a company, but without a company the investment must be spent on the purchase of products, real estate or employee's salaries.

## Netherlands

For a foreign investor to get a residence permit in the Netherlands, a minimum capital investment of € 27,000 is required along with the following qualifications:
- No older than 60 years of age.
- A business person must own more than 20 percent of the company.
- A monthly income of at least € 1,400.
- The application can include a spouse, unmarried partner and children under the age of 18.

## New Zealand

New Zealand is another country that offers two options for foreign investors, both of which offer permanent residency. For the Investor Visa an investor must:

- Be under the age of 65.
- Have at least three years business experience.
- Meet English language requirements.
- Make an investment of $1.5 million NZ for a period of five years.
- Demonstrate the intention and ability to settle in New Zealand.

The other option is the Investor Plus Visa which as no language, age or experience requirements, but has an increased $10 million NZ investment over a three year period.

## Portugal

A foreign investor can get a Golden Visa allowing them to live in Portugal for five years. The visa can be extended to family members including children, spouse and dependent family members. The residency permit is offered for an initial one year period and is then renewed in two-year periods. After five years, an application can be placed for permanent residency. Applicants need to have a total of € 500,000 in property investments in Portugal, make a transfer of at least € 1 million or create a minimum of ten jobs with the investment.

## South Korea

In order to live in South Korea, foreign investors must apply for a D-8 Residence Visa. Applicants for this visa need to establish a company in South Korea or enter a partnership with a Korean firm and invest a minimum of 100 million won. Those who get a D-8 Visa and have made the required investment can also apply for an F-5 Visa after living in the country for at least five years and creating at least three employment opportunities. The F-5 Visa allows for permanent residency. This visa is offered to foreign investors, high level professionals and directors of multinational corporations. For this visa, applicants must invest the minimum amount of funds and hire a minimum of five Korean nationals.

## Spain

Spain offers foreign investors permanent residency through the Spanish Investor Residency Visa. The initial permit is valid for two years, after which the investor can apply for a renewal of an additional two years. Then after five years, the investor can apply for permanent residency. The qualifications for this visa include:

- A minimum investment of € 500,000 in residential real estate.
- A minimum age of 18.
- No criminal record in Spain or other residence countries.
- Sufficient funds to support both the applicant and their immediate family members during the time they reside in Spain.

Switzerland

The Swiss Resident Program has one main advantage for foreign investors immigrating to Switzerland compared to other high tax countries. Investors need a minimum of $250,000 USD at their disposal before they can apply. Upon paying an "annual lump sum taxation" fee that can be a minimum of 150,000 CHF up to 1 million CHF, the investor is then issued a residence permit. Upon paying this lump sum taxation, there is no need to declare worldwide income and assets. It can typically take three to four months to obtain a residence permit. Eligibility requirements include:
- A minimum age of 18.
- Not currently employed or living in Switzerland.
- Must be the investor's first time living in Switzerland.
- The investor must rent or purchase a residence in Switzerland.

- Provide a list of identification documents including a clean criminal record and good moral character.

## United Kingdom

Foreign investors can apply for a Tier 1 Investor Visa in the United Kingdom with which they can remain in status for about three years and then they need to apply for an extension if they want to continue living in the United Kingdom. The investors need personal assets that value over £2 million and have at least £1 million of their own money in the country. A minimum investment of £750,000 must be made through U.K. government bonds, share capital or investment capital in an active U.K. company. Depending on the investment amount, a visa holder needs residency of two, three or five years in order to apply for permanent residency.

# United States and Birth of EB-5 Visa

In the United States, the USCIS administers the EB-5 visa program. This program was created by Congress in 1990 in order to stimulate the economy in the United States through job creation and capital investment through foreign investors. Foreign investors can also get an EB-5 visa by investing through regional centers designated by USCIS based on specific proposals for promoting economic growth. Before I get into specifics about the program and how you can apply for an EB-5 visa, let's take a look at the history of the program.

## EB-5 Program History

The EB-5, also known as the Immigrant Investor Program, was created as a part of the United States Congress' Immigration Act of 1990. This act was responsible for significantly restructuring the U.S. immigration system; including major changes to the non-immigrant visa categories, deportation rules and increased legal immigration limits. The EB-5 program was started by Congress as a way to stimulate the economy in the United States by allow foreign investors to have the opportunity to permanently live and work in the United States after investing in a United States commercial enterprise.

In 1993, the Immigrant Investor Pilot Program was created by Congress in order to increase interest in the EB-5 program. Under this pilot program, EB-5 Regional Centers were established. These regional centers are business entities that have a special designation from USCIS (United States Citizenship and Immigration Service) to administer investments and create jobs. We'll discuss more about these regional centers later.

In the late 1990s, several major overhauls were made to the EB-5 program. These changes were the result of lax regulation enforcement and fraud discovered within EB-5 investments. The case of U.S. v. O'Connor in the U.S. District Court was a ruling that helped to uncover fraudulent EB-5 investment schemes. The appeals unit of USCIS, the Administrative Appeals Office (AAO), issued changes to the EB-5 requirements in 1998. The changes required foreign investors to prove that EB-5 investments were coming from lawful sources and that the foreign investors were personally involved in their EB-5 project. The changes also prohibited investment return guarantees. When the USCIS tried to apply these regulations retroactively to former EB-5 cases, the ruling of Chang v. U.S. made this illegal. Once the new regulations took effect the number of EB-5 applicants dropped significantly.

The AAO now has the job of making sure that EB-5 regulations are uniformly applied to any new application. Because of this, there were four very important precedent decisions in the 1990s: Matter of Ho, Matter of Hsiung, Matter of Izummi and Matter of Soffici. All of these precedents are still binding for current applications. From these precedents, the AAO made determinations on the requirements including the type of commercial entity for EB-5 investment, the qualifications for legal sources of funding and how an investment can be administered.

In order to revitalize the EB-5 program, Congress passed the Basic Pilot Program Extension and Expansion Act of 2003. Under this act, the Government Accounting Office (GAO) conducted a thorough investigation into the EB-5 program. The investigation found that only a fraction of the allocated 10,000 visas were actually being granted each year. As a result of these findings, more reforms were prompted. One of these reforms led to the creation of the Investor and Regional Center Unit (IRCU) in 2005. This specialty unit was given oversight of the EB-5 program including things such as case auditing, form design, regulation development and policy creation. Once the IRCU was formed the EB-5 program developed better coordination and increased reliability.

In 2009, the USCIS issued revised policy guidance for the EB-5. EB-5 processing was centralized at the California Service Center (CSC) when the processing had previously been done at two different centers in both California and Texas. Even though the EB-5 program is not permanent yet, it has been consistently reauthorized. President Obama extended the EB-5 pilot program until September 30, 2012 and then reauthorized a three year extension until 2015. The EB-5 program continues today with some very specific requirements. Let's first take a quick look at what these requirements are.

# 3 Main Requirements of EB-5 Visa

In order to obtain permanent residency through the EB-5 visa program, a foreign investor needs to meet specific requirements specified by the United States Citizenship and Immigration (USCIS). In general these requirements center around capital investment amount requirements, job creation requirements and ensure that the business receiving the investment qualifies under the EB-5 program. Once all the requirements are made an applicant, their spouse and any children under the age of 21 will obtain permanent residency green cards.

## Business Entity Requirements

A foreign investor can invest in several types of business entities while applying for an EB-5 visa. The foreign investors can either directly invest in a new commercial enterprise or in a regional center.

A new commercial enterprise needs to be a lawful for-profit entity. The business structure can include:
- Corporations
- Holding Companies
- Joint Ventures
- Limited or General Partnerships
- Sole Proprietorships

- Business Trusts
- Privately or Publicly Owned Business Structures

All new commercial enterprises need to have been established after November 29, 1990. An older commercial enterprise can qualify if the investment leads to a 40 percent increase in the number of employees or net worth or if the older business is restructured to the point that a new commercial enterprise results. EB-5 visa applicants can also invest in an EB-5 Regional Center. The advantages for an investor to choose a regional center run project is because the investor won't have to independently set up an EB-5 project.

## Job Creation Requirements

It is also a requirement that all EB-5 investments result in the creation or preservation of ten full-time jobs for U.S. workers. These jobs need to be created within a two year period of the investor being awarded a conditional permanent residency. The jobs must be either direct or indirect. Direct jobs are identifiable jobs for employees who work directly within the business that is receiving the investment. If the foreign investor created the investment through a regional center, then indirect or induced jobs will also qualify. These are jobs created collaterally or as a result of the capital invested. For example, an indirect job would be those created in a business that supplies goods or services to the EB-5 project and induced jobs are those that are created within the greater community as a result of income spent by EB-5 employees.

Investors can only count preserved jobs if they are assisting a troubled business. A troubled business is a company that has been around for at least two years and has a net loss during the 12 or 24 month period prior to the priority date on the immigrant investor's Form I-526. The loss during this period needs to be at least 20 percent of the troubled business' net worth before the loss.

A qualified employee can include a U.S. Citizen, permanent resident or other immigrant that is authorized to work within the United States. It can also include a conditional resident, a refugee or a person residing under suspension of deportation. The number can't include the investor, his family, or any foreign national in any non-immigrant status or those who are not authorized to work within the United States.

The jobs created must be full-time employment. This means that qualifying employees must be in a position that requires at least 35 working hours per week. Under the pilot program, full-time employment can also include employees in positions created indirectly from investments that come from the pilot program. Full-time employment can also include a condition known as job-sharing arrangement. This is where two or more qualifying employees share a full-time position. However, this doesn't include combinations of part-time positions or full-time equivalents even if they meet the hourly requirement per week. The employment position needs to be permanent, full-time and constant.

## Capital Investment Requirements

Those applying for an EB-5 visa are typically required to make a capital investment of either $500,000 or $1 million in a U.S. commercial enterprise. The investment can be made in several forms:

- Cash
- Inventory
- Equipment
- Secured Indebtedness
- Tangible Property
- Cash Equivalents based on U.S. dollar fair-market value.

The foreign investors must be personally and primarily liable and any assets cannot be used to secure any of the indebtedness. All capital must come from lawful sources and cannot be borrowed.

The investment can only be reduced to $500,000 if the commercial entity is located within a targeted employment area (TEA). A TEA designation is given to a rural area or an area that has high unemployment. High unemployment is determined as an unemployment rate that is at least 150 percent of the national unemployment rate at the time of investment. Rural areas are region outside of a city with a population of 20,000 or more.

## 5 Steps to Getting an EB-5 Visa

As a foreign investor, if you want to get an EB-5 visa there are five steps you need to complete. Each of these steps involves a lot of work and research to make the right decisions. However, all of your work will pay off in the end because you will be able to become a permanent resident of the United States along with your spouse and any unmarried children until the age of 21. Let's consider each of these steps to make them easier for you.

## Step-1: Choosing an EB-5 Project

The first step you need to take is to find a suitable business project to invest in. As a foreign investor, there are two paths you can take when it comes to investing in an EB-5 project: you can invest directly or you can invest through a regional center project. Often there are overseas agents that will help EB-5 investors determine the best project for their needs. Although, if you want to make this decision on your own let's consider each option available.

**Direct Investment vs. Regional Center Investment**

### The Basics of Direct Investment

If you choose the direct investment method then you will be investing directly into an enterprise rather than through an intermediary. For this option the required minimum investment is one million USD unless the business is located in a targeted employment area (TEA), which would make the minimum investment requirement $500,000. When choosing this option you will also be required to prove on your visa petition that your investment is directly creating full-time jobs for at least ten qualifying employees within two years of getting your visa approved. Direct jobs are actual and identifiable jobs through W-2 forms and are located within the company you are investing in. In addition to these two main requirements, you will also need to meet other legal requirements such as those related to the establishment of a new commercial enterprise, engagement in investor management and if needed application for a location as a TEA.

## What is an EB-5 Business?

Since you are making a sizable investment, it is important that you completely understand all the components of the EB-5 program. The most important part of this process that can determine your success or failure is the selection of the right EB-5 business or project.

EB-5 businesses are often funded through regional centers, with nearly 90 to 95 percent of all applicants for the EB-5 program investing through regional centers. However, you can choose to direct your required capital investment to your own EB-5 business or project. If you are going to do this you need to make sure it is a new commercial enterprise and that it will lead to the creation of at least 10 full-time jobs for U.S. workers.

A new commercial enterprise must be a lawful, for profit business that was started after November 29, 1990. An older business would only qualify for an EB-5 investment if it was significantly restructured or if the number of employees or net worth was increased by over 40 percent. The businesses can be structured as a sole proprietorship, limited or general partnership, corporation, business trust or other publicly or privately owned business.

## Types of EB-5 Businesses

An EB-5 project can encompass a variety of business models and operate within numerous industries. Some EB-5 projects to consider include the following:

- Agricultural developments such as farms and wineries.
- Biotech and medical technology.
- Casinos.
- Convention centers.
- Electric vehicles.
- Entertainment venues.
- Hotels.
- Manufacturing.
- Mixed use retail.
- Office buildings.
- Restaurants.
- Sports stadiums.

## Tips for Choosing an EB-5 Business

As you can tell from the list above, it can be quite a challenge to choose a project to invest in for your EB-5 visa. However, the most important step in the EB-5 process is to choose a project that both meets USCIS criteria and is a viable business option. Your permanent residency in the United States is dependent on you being able to choose a project that creates jobs and adheres to USCIS criteria. While you may be drawn to a particular project because you are familiar with the industry or location of the project, there are a few due diligence questions that you need to consider before determining where to invest your money. Take the time to consider your answers to the following questions:

- Are there other EB-5 investors already committed to the project?
- If so, where are the other EB-5 investors in the visa application process?
- What are the risks associated with the project?
- What are the projected returns on the investment?
- Does the project require non EB-5 funding?
- If so, where do these funds come from?
- Will the investment and related fees be refunded if the I-526 petition is denied?
- What are the industries within the regional center's USCIS designation?
- Does the project fit within these designations or do you need to file an amendment?

- What EB-5 experience do the regional center's immigration and securities counsel have?
- What is the screening process for potential investors?
- Have the regional center or project principles ever been involved in a lawsuit or bankruptcy?
- What are the credentials of the project's principles?
- What economic or econometric models are used to forecast the required number of jobs to be created?
- How are jobs created?
- How are jobs allocated among investors?
- Is the business project's plan compliant with Matter of Ho? ( <u>Matter of Ho</u> is as part of an I-526 petition an EB-5 investor must submit a comprehensive business plan)
- Does the project qualify for the lowered $500,000 investment requirement because it is located in a high unemployment or rural area?
- What is the exit strategy from the project upon receipt of permanent residency?

You should never feel pressured to choose one project over another. Make sure you take the time to do your homework and choose your EB-5 project carefully. However, if this seems like too much then there is another option available.

Regional Center Investment

If you choose to invest through the regional center option, then you are investing in an enterprise through a government-approved regional center. The minimum investment amount is still $1 million or $500,000 if the regional center is located in a TEA. It should be noted that the majority of regional centers are located in TEAs. The difference with a regional center investment versus a direct investment is the fact that as a regional center investor your job creation requirement can be both direct and indirect. Indirect jobs are those created as a result of the regional center's dispersal of investments to new commercial enterprises. In addition, since regional centers are pre-approved by the government to promote economic growth; investing in a regional center means you won't have to conduct independent investigations and analysis in order to prove in your visa petition that the job creation requirement has been met, that a new commercial enterprise has been established or that the investor is engaged in the management of the business.

**What is an EB-5 Regional Center?**

An EB-5 Regional Center is an organization designated by the United States Citizenship and Immigration Services (USCIS) that sponsors capital investment projects for EB-5 investors. Regional centers are helpful for EB-5 investors because they reduce the difficulty of meeting the qualifications under EB-5 program rules.

The Regional Center (RC) can be used by both investors and companies looking to complete a project through the EB-5 program. The regional center can be established by any private or public economic entity that is focused on increasing domestic capital, job creation, improved regional productivity and increased economic growth. A regional center is a good option for those who are more focused on obtaining a green card rather than directly managing an investment.

The regional center is one of two ways that an EB-5 investor can choose when it comes to obtaining permanent residence; the other option is the direct investment route discussed above. Rather in investing directly into the project, the regional center sets up an investment fund for the benefit of all EB-5 investors. Investors can then purchase equity stakes in the investment fund. The fund is then used to either purchase equity in the job creating entity or loans the job creating entity money. The investment is then used to fund the project to create jobs indirectly.

## Forming a Regional Center

A regional center needs to apply for designation by filing a

Form I-924 with the USCIS. Once approved, the USCIS will designate the RC to develop capital investment projects within a specific geographic area and for a specific industry. The RC is also specifically designated to use specific economic methodologies to model indirect job creation.

You can also choose to start your own regional center. To do this you must provide the USCIS with a hypothetical project or an actual ready project. Along with the application for a regional center you will be in a good position for an I-526 petition to get project pre-approval for an actual project through which EB-5 immigrants make investments. With a good I-526 petition you will be able to speed up the process for additional I-526 petitions filed by investors in the project.
Let's take a moment to look at these two options closely.

How to Use a Regional Center for Investment

In recent years, the EB-5 regional center has gained in popularity. Although the EB-5 visa program has been around since the 1990s, it has only recently seen a surge in interest during the recession in the economy. Many developers, entrepreneurs, businesses and even some municipalities found themselves struggling for cash and viewed the EB-5 program as a way to get the capital required for a number of projects. Regional centers were viewed as a convenient and easy way to get the capital needed at a fraction of the cost of traditional investment sources in the United States.

However, along with this increase in popularity; the USCIS was also faced with a number of issues that they hadn't previously needed to address. Initially the program seemed to be an efficient way to get capital, but it had become a long, convoluted and expensive process. Sometimes an application for a regional center could take up to two years to process. This extended processing time caused many developers and entrepreneurs to look for creative ways to use the regional center program without having to wait out the prolonged processing time. As a result many entrepreneurs decided to purchase, collaborate and/or rent existing regional centers rather than establish new ones. Therefore, one of the popular options today is to rent a regional center.

Renting a regional center is a good alternative to establishing your own regional center. While this may seem like a good option for most, the transactions can have negative impacts for both the regional center and the renter if the process isn't executed properly. However, renting a regional center is a good option for those who want to use foreign investment in order to develop their projects. If you choose to rent a regional center you need to take precautions and use due diligence in order to make sure the transaction is successful. Consider the following 6 steps in order to have a successful rental of a regional center.

## 1, Identify the Regional Center

The first step in renting a regional center is to find one that meets your specific needs. There are three questions you need to ask when making sure you are choosing the right regional center:

- What are the geographic limitations of the regional center and does it accommodate your project?
- What are the approved North American Industry Classification System (NAICS) codes?
- Do the codes work for your project or do you need to get an amendment?

The best way to get an answer to these three questions is to request a copy of the USCIS approval letter from the regional center. This can help you determine the geographical and industry scope of the regional center you are considering. Keep in mind that you need to rent a regional center that will allow you to immediately start your project.

## 2. Due Diligence

If you are going to rent a regional center it is important to conduct your due diligence. As with any company you do business with, you want to investigate the background of the company. If a regional center has been in business for any period of time then they have likely been exposed to some level of liability. Again, as with a business partner, you won't want to start a project with a regional center that has a lot of liability or worse, impending litigation.

There are at least five things to include in your due diligence:
- Review the regional center application.
- Search for any current or pending litigation.
- Research the background of any principals.
- Review all offerings.
- Review the success of the offerings.

## 3. Approvals of Forms I-526 / I-829

A regional center won't do you any good if it isn't able to get the Forms I-526 and I-829 approved. Therefore, if you are going to rent a regional center, then you need to find out how many of these forms it has had approved. If the regional center has had more denials than approvals you may want to reconsider renting with the specific regional center.

## 4. Compliance

Along with form completion, it is important to make sure that the regional center complies with all state and federal laws. If you are going to use the EB-5 program you need to understand that you are dealing with several different areas of law and while the regional center may be compliant in one area doesn't mean it is compliant in all areas. Therefore, you need to make sure you retain experts in all areas of the law to make sure the regional center is compliant.

## 5. Negotiate Terms

After all your research in the first four steps is complete, you now need to negotiate the terms of the contract. There are three important points to consider when negotiating a contract:

First, the most important part is determining how much it will cost to rent the regional center. Negotiate for upfront fees, know what the regional center will charge per investor and determine if they require an equity stake in the project. You should do a thorough cost benefit analysis in order to ensure the venture will be profitable for all involved. Some regional centers will have high upfront fees and an equity interest in the project; so you should make sure it is a profitable proposition. You also want to make sure you know what the regional center's obligations will be under the contract. While a lot of these details may seem minor, failure to address these early on in the negotiating process can cause significant expenses later.

Second, it is important that you discuss the level of oversight the regional center will have over the project. This will also help to give you a positive indicator of the regional center's compliance.

Third, determine the level of competition you will be facing from within the regional center itself. If the regional center rents itself out often, make sure there are no similar current or pending projects in the works. You may want to negotiate for a non-compete for the duration of the project, this way the regional center won't be able to rent out to other entrepreneurs.

6. Contract

Lastly, the most important step is to put everything together as a contract. The contract should be drafted in a manner that clearly reflects the agreement and understanding of all parties involved. While the transaction can be structured in a number of ways; it is best to structure it like a "licensing" agreement with focus being placed on the indemnification clause to make sure you aren't facing any liability that the regional center may have incurred before.

When you structure things properly, renting a regional center may be a very cost efficient option. It will allow you to utilize foreign capital without having to start your own regional center. But let's take the time to consider the second option in case you decide to go that way instead.

## Why Become a Regional Center?

There are many advantages to receiving an EB-5 Regional Center designation from USCIS. It can be a way for a business project to raise low interest debt and sometimes equity. Getting capital through the EB-5 program is quite different from other traditional funding sources. The EB-5 program is an exciting and ever changing industry.

Starting in 2007, the EB-5 program increased in popularity when traditional lending became more difficult. When it comes to EB-5 capital it can be done through direct investment or investment through a regional center. The option of going through a regional center is more attractive since it makes some USCIS requirements less stringent for EB-5 visa applicants. Regional centers have less stringent job creation requirements than a direct investment. The regional center is also able to enjoy the benefit of economic multipliers when creating new jobs. Regional centers also make it easier to pool capital since there are no limits on the EB-5 applicants who can invest in a project, so long as the job creation requirements are met. However, your specific needs will determine whether or not a regional center is an advantageous way of investing.

## How to Become a Regional Center

Pretty much anyone can apply for designation for a regional center without any special licenses being required. Regional center is a term that can be applied to any economic unit whether public or private that is involved in the promotion of economic growth; including increased export sales, improved regional productivity, job creation and increased domestic capital investment. The business models that are able to become regional centers include government agencies, partnerships, corporations and any existing commercial entity in the United States.

To become a regional center you need to get approval from USCIS. To do this you need to follow a multi-step process that involves the input of various experts. The costs of getting approved as a regional center can vary. The actual application through the Application for Regional Center under the Immigrant Investor Program petition costs $6,230 to file. However, the cost is often a lot higher depending on the fees charged by the various experts involved.

## Steps to Become an EB-5 Regional Center

In order to get EB-5 Regional Center approval from USCIS, there are a few steps you must take. The readiness of your project will determine the costs involved and the documents required. When you file for regional center status you need to accompany it with a project. The USCIS recognizes three categories for project readiness: hypothetical, actual and exemplar.

Hypothetical projects are proposals that aren't supported by a Matter of Ho compliant business plan. Often the general proposals and predictions of this sample project will be enough to determine if the proposed regional center will be able to promote economic growth.

Actual projects have a little more detail than hypothetical projects. The proposal needs to contain verifiable details that are supported by economically or statistically sound forecasting tools. This often means there is a comprehensive business plan and economic report that describes the project, investment, job creation, etc.

Exemplar projects have a Form I-526 petition, filed with a Form I-924 actual project proposal. These projects need to have a copy of the commercial enterprise's organizational and transactional documents. The USCIS will review all the documents to make sure they comply with EB-5 eligibility requirements. Let's look at the steps required for each category and what additional documents may be needed.

Determine the Scope

The first and most important step in the approval process is for the business organization to determine their geographic scope and economic benefit. This includes defining a geographic umbrella, business industry focus, corporate structure, operational business model and required investment amount for the regional center and any potential project.

Hire Professional Services for Regional Center Filing

The following are the minimum documents required for each project category level:

For a hypothetical project: Regional Center Operational Business Plan, Corporate Structure agreements for ownership of the regional center, sample project business plan, economist report for the project and sample management agreement between the regional center and the project.

For an actual project the documents above are required along with a comprehensive project business plan and sample transactional documents, often an investor subscription agreement and private placement memorandum.

For an exemplar project all the documents listed above are required along with final transactional documents along with a sample Form I-526 Immigration Petition by Alien Entrepreneur.

Business Plan Writer

The first expert to contact is a business plan writer who has knowledge of producing EB-5 compliant business plans since the business plan is one of the most important documents required for filing for regional center status. The AAO precedent decision known as Matter of Ho has set the standards by which the USCIS will review business plans. The plan should include the following:
- Market analysis, including the names of competing businesses and their strengths and weaknesses.
- A comparison of the competition's products and pricing structures.

- A description of the target market/prospective customers of the new commercial enterprise.
- Required permits and licenses obtained.
- A description of manufacturing or production processes, the materials required and the supply sources.
- Any contracts executed for the supply of materials and/or the distribution of products.
- Business marketing strategy including pricing, advertising and servicing.
- Business organizational structure and personnel experience.
- Staffing requirements and timetable for hiring, as well as job descriptions for all positions.
- Sales, cost and income projections and detail the bases.

## Economist

The next most important expert to hire is an economist. These individuals are responsible for preparing a job calculation and job creation report. These expert reports are important because regional centers are allowed to use both indirect and induced job creation numbers. Indirect jobs can qualify based on reasonable economic methodologies, even if they are outside of a regional center's geographical boundaries. When it comes to demonstrating indirect job creation, petitioners need to employ reasonable economic methodologies in order to establish a preponderance of evidence that the required infusion of capital or creation of direct jobs will result in a specific number of indirect jobs. An economist will also determine if a regional center will be located within a targeted employment area (TEA).

## Securities Counsel

As with the business writer you want to make sure you hire a securities counsel that has experience in producing EB-5 compliant subscription and private placement memorandums. The documents need to comply not only with Security and Exchange Commission federal regulations, but also USCIS regulations. The most important is the "at risk" requirement: in order for an investment to be qualified under the EB-5 program, the immigrant investor need to actually place their capital "at risk" in order to generate a return; the mere intent to invest isn't enough. The foreign investor must show actual commitment in the form of the required amount of capital. This means that any clause providing a put, call or redemption of investment funds prior to final adjudication of Form I-829 Petition by Entrepreneur to Remove Conditions will result in a possible denial of the application.

## I-924 Petition

Once you have all the required documents in place, then you can submit an I-924 petition to the USCIS. After this form is filed, the regional center can go to market and advertise the project. However, the regional center cannot accept any investment from a foreign investor until the regional center is approved.

The I-924 is required for a regional center to operate legally. After the application is approved, regional center designation is granted and the regional center can start receiving foreign capital investment in order to fund EB-5 projects.

An I-924 can also be filed by an existing regional center that wants to amend their original designation or to gain exemplar, project pre-approval. Amendments can include changes to the geographical area, organizational structure or investment project business plans / NAICS code designations.

## I-924 Requirements

Multiple pieces of evidence need to be submitted along with the I-924 application. The forms of required evidence will vary depending on the actual EB-5 project. But in general you will need the following:

Since the regional center must focus on a particular geographic location, a detailed map of the proposed regional center location is required.

Each EB-5 investor needs to prove ten full time jobs will be created. This is provided through the following documents:
- Economic Report
- Business Plan
- Financial Projections / Pro Formas demonstrating how funds will be spent
- SEC / offering documents including private placement memorandum
- Subscription agreement
- Due diligence questionnaires / accredited investor questionnaires
- LP or LLC agreement for the EB-5 investment vehicle

A description of the promotional activities of the regional center requires the following documents:
- Detailed description of past, current and future promotional activities.
- Budgets for promotional activities.
- Evidence of funds that have been allocated to promotional activities.

- Marketing and operational plan of how the regional center will attract investors.
- Description of how the regional center will ensure that all investments come from lawful sources.

Proof is also required that the regional center will be compliant with all EB-5 regulations which is done through the following documents:
- Documentation of the business structure of both the regional center and the new commercial enterprises that are affiliated with the regional center which can include articles of incorporation.
- Drafts of investment agreements.
- Escrow agreement.
- Investment offering letter.
- Contracts, agreements or memorandums made with organizations that will engage in activities on behalf of the regional center.

## Filing I-924

The application is typically filed by immigration attorneys with the help of others including corporate and securities attorneys, economists, accountants and business plan writers. The filing fee for the application is $6,230. The application is submitted through the USCIS California Service Center. Processing time typically takes between four and ten months, but can take longer. Sometimes the USCIS will require additional information from the applicant. The regional center will also need to file an I-924A Supplement for each fiscal year after initial approval. This supplement will help the regional center prove that is has followed all program regulations and is still eligible for designation as a regional center.

I-526 Petitions

After the I-924 is approved, the regional center can then submit the Form I-526 petitions from the EB-5 investors. The I-526 applications are used to outline specific EB-5 projects that the regional center is going to be doing and will include either the documents discussed above in the actual or exemplar filing. While the Form I-526 is a self petition by each individual investor, it is important to have the expert services of an immigration counsel on site. Immigration counsel can help review and guide the regional center, project and investor through all the compliance steps of the USCIS. After the I-526 petitions are approved, the individual EB-5 investors will receive their conditional green card that allows them to move to the United States.

Form I-526

The EB-5 investor needs to file the I-526 Immigrant Petition by Alien Entrepreneur in order to demonstrate that they are in the process of investing or have already invested the proper amount of capital in an approved EB-5 project. An immigration attorney can also prepare an I-526 petition on behalf of the EB-5 applicant. Any applicant is eligible for file an I-526 once they have taken the necessary measures to invest in an approved EB-5 project. These projects must be attached to a new commercial enterprise and can be done either directly through the immigrant investor or done through a regional center, which has the government designation to administer EB-5 projects.

Along with the petition, an investor must provide proof that they have made a $500,000 to $1 million U.S. Dollar investment of lawful capital into a new commercial enterprise. The specific investment will depend on whether the investment is made within an economically depressed area known as a targeted employment area (TEA). The main focus of the I-526 petition is that the applicants have to prove that their capital investment comes from legal sources of funds. Therefore, proof must be given that the funds were legally obtained via traceable evidence.

An applicant also needs to provide necessary proof that their investment is going to lead to the creation of at least ten full-time jobs for U.S. Citizens, permanent residents or other authorized immigrant workers. Another item of proof that is required is evidence that shows the EB-5 investor will be in either a policymaking or managerial role of the EB-5 project. This proof can be met by demonstrating that an investor has voting rights in an EB-5 project in the form of a limited partnership or limited liability company.

## I-526 Requirements

In addition to the ones discussed above, there are many other pieces of evidence that can be used to provide proof that the I-526 petition requirements have been met. Consider what some of your other options may be:

You need to prove that an approved EB-5 project has received or will receive the investment. Proof of this can include the following:
- Articles of incorporation
- Merger or consolidation certificates
- Joint venture or limited partnership agreements
- State business certificates

Proof is also required to show that the appropriate investment amount has been made into the approved EB-5 project. This can be done through the following documents:
- Bank statements
- Security agreements

- Promissory notes
- Loan or mortgage certificates
- Other evidence that sufficiently illustrates the investment amount

Just showing the amount isn't enough, you will also need proof that these funds came from a lawful and legal source. This can be done with the following documents:

- Five years of tax returns
- Pay stubs of the funds coming from earnings from an employer
- Bank account statements
- Securities statements if the funds are coming from trading/bonds/stocks

Then there is the need to prove that the investment will lead to the creation of at least ten full time jobs. The only evidence of this is through a solid business plan.

Lastly, you will need to provide proof that you will be involved in the day-to-day management of the EB-5 project or will at least have a policy-making position. This is done through one of two documents; either corporate documents or a statement and description of duties.

## Filing the I-526

Typically an immigration attorney will be the one to file the I-526 petition. They are submitted through the USCIS California Service Center with a filing fee of $1,500. Sometimes the USCIS will request additional proof. A finding of whether or not the petition is approved will be given in about five to ten months. After the petition is complete then the EB-5 visa applicant can apply for U.S. Residential status by filing the Form I-485 adjustment of status if they are already in the United States or by filing the DS-230 if they are still living abroad.

## Administer EB-5 Project and Stay in Compliance with the USCIS

Once the regional center is approved you work doesn't end. You still need to keep track of your investors and monitor job creation requirements for each project. An annual compliance report, Form I-924a, is required by the USCIS. The regional center also needs to make filings with the Securities and Exchange Commission as well as any other state and local agency that regulates securities.

### I-829 Petitions by EB-5 Visa Applicants

The last step in creating a regional center is to have each individual investor to file the I-829 petition. This petition demonstrates that the project and investor have met all the

EB-5 program requirements. After this petition is approved, the investor is able to gain lawful permanent resident status or green card in the United States. While the petition is filed by the individual applicant, the regional center is responsible for providing the proof that the job creation requirements have been met as a result of the investment.

## Advantages of a Regional Center Investment

The biggest advantage to going through a regional center for your investment is that the USCIS will allow the EB-5 project to count both direct and indirect or induced jobs when considering the job creation requirement. This is easier since a direct job is an actual identifiable job for a qualified employee within the commercial enterprise that the EB-5 investor is investing in; whereas indirect jobs are those that can be shown to be created collaterally by the project as a result of investment in the new commercial enterprise through an affiliated regional center. In addition, induced jobs are jobs created within the community where the regional center is as a result of income spent by EB-5 project workers. The actual number of indirect jobs you are able to count will depend upon your business plan and a detailed economic analysis that the USCIS will evaluate and approve when the regional center files for approval and designation under the Immigrant Investor Pilot Program.

Another advantage is that investors going through an affiliated regional center for their new commercial enterprise won't have to prove they are involved in the day-to-day management of the business. Rather an EB-5 investor can simply be involved in the policy formation of the funds. Often this requires the funding of a new commercial enterprise to be organized as a limited partnership or limited liability company. The EB-5 investor can become a limited partner or member and still get all the benefits of the State's Uniform Limited Partnership Act or Limited Liability Company Act. These rights are sufficient to prove involvement when qualifying for an EB-5 visa through a regional center. This means you won't need to commit a specific amount of time in directing the business. This is good for those whose goal is simply to get a green card through the EB-5 program. For others, if they want to control the business then it may be a better idea to go through the direct investment route.

Many EB-5 investors also prefer the regional center investment model because they can live anywhere in the United States. You don't necessarily have to live by the project you are funding. It also gives you the freedom to work anywhere since your employment isn't tied to the new commercial enterprise or the EB-5 project. The EB-5 visa will also allow your dependents to move permanently to the

United States and this allows them to go to school or work anywhere in the United States without restrictions.

## Regional Center Statistics

Currently there are 325 USCIS approved EB-5 regional centers throughout the United States and more are regularly being approved. In comparison, there were only 27 regional centers back in 2008. Regional centers are allowed to operate multiple EB-5 projects simultaneously so they can receive funding from multiple EB-5 investors as long as the job creation requirements are met so that they can accumulate more capital for the projects.

## Step -2: Meet Job Creation Requirements

The EB-5 investor visa is overseen by the United States Citizenship and Immigration Service under the Immigrant Investor Program. The EB-5 visa is classified as an employment based fifth preference visa. In order to get an EB-5 visa, a foreign investor or entrepreneur needs to meet specific requirements. One of these requirements is to preserve or create a minimum of ten full-time positions for qualified United States workers.

The preservation or creating of these jobs need to happen before the investor files their I-526 or can prove through a business plan that the job will be created or preserved within the first two years of conditional permanent residency. The jobs do need to be maintained during this two year period until the filing of the I-829 can remove these conditions.

The jobs created for an EB-5 project can be broken down as direct, indirect or induced jobs. In some instances, an applicant for an EB-5 visa will need to prove that their capital resulted in the direct creation of jobs for employees working directly for the business in which the investment was made.

## Job Requirements for Regional Centers and Direct Investments

In 1992 the Immigrant Investor Pilot Program created EB-5 regional centers. These economic units are allowed by the USCIS to count both direct and indirect jobs towards the requirements for the EB-5 program.

A regional center can be either a public or private entity that improves the productivity of a region, promotes economic growth, increases domestic capital investment and increases job creation. The USCIS must designate a regional center and has specific criteria for them such as the demonstration through economic models of how EB-5 capital will be able to create jobs and how the regional center will be able to positively impact the region or the U.S. Economy as a whole.

The ability to count indirect and induced jobs along with direct jobs is one of the major benefits of using an EB-5 regional center. On the other hand, if you are going to directly invest in an EB-5 project then the ten full-time jobs created must be within the business itself that received the investment.

## Direct Jobs

A direct job is an actual identifiable position for a qualified US worker and employee. These jobs are created within the business enterprise itself, the one that the foreign investor places their EB-5 capital per the program requirements. The direct job must be a full time position; that means at least 35 work hours a week. An alternative to this full time position would be a job sharing option. With this arrangement, employees who qualify would divide the hours of a single full time position among themselves. This way the same amount of hours that would normally be worked by a single full time employee is split among the individuals under a job sharing agreement. However, part time jobs are not combined to meet the job requirements; even if they equal the same amount of hours as a full time position when added together.

## Indirect Jobs

Indirect jobs are those that can be found in businesses and commercial enterprises associated or affiliated with an EB-5 regional center. These jobs must be shown to have been created as a result of the capital invested by the foreign investor. The USCIS will usually only count indirect jobs towards the job creation requirement if they are a part of an EB-5 investment through an USCIS designated regional centers. These types of jobs are typically found in businesses that supply goods or services to an EB-5 project.

### Induced Jobs

Induced jobs are those created in the community in which the regional center has geographical coverage. The creation of induced jobs can be attributed to increased spending by those involved in an EB-5 project.

### Qualified Employee

The definition of a qualified employee by the USCIS is an individual who has work authorization in the United States. This can mean either a citizen or a permanent resident of the United States. In addition, a qualified employee can mean any of the following:

- Persons under suspension of deportation currently living in the United States
- Conditional residents
- Refugees
- Asylees

Those who don't qualify as employees for the purpose of the job creation requirements for an EB-5 investment include the following:

- Those who don't have authorization to work in the

United States
- The foreign investor applying for an EB-5 visa
- The foreign investor's family
- Foreign national living in the United States with a non-immigrant status

## Troubled Businesses

The USCIS will also allow EB-5 applicants to count preserved jobs if they are dealing with a troubled business. A trouble business is defined by the USCIS as an enterprise that experienced a net loss for a minimum of two years. The next loss needs to have occurred during a 12 to 24 month period before the priority date on the EB-5 applicant's I-526 petition. Also the net loss must equal a minimum of 20 percent of the enterprise's value before the loss started.

## Targeted Employment Area

An important thing for an EB-5 investor is to get an EB-5 project awarded a targeted employment area (TEA) designation. When this occurs the required investment amount is lowered from $1 million to $500,000 dollars when the EB-5 project takes place in a targeted employment area. For a TEA designation to be granted, the EB-5 project needs to be either located in a rural area or in a place that has a high unemployment rate. A TEA designation is requested when the EB-5 investor submits their I-526 petition. When you invest in a regional center they will notify you if any of their projects are located within a TEA.

## What is a Rural Area?

An EB-5 project location needs to meet specific criteria in order to qualify as a TEA rural area. The rural area cannot be within a metropolitan statistical area as labeled by the U.S. Office of Management and Budget. The rural area also cannot be located on the outskirts of a city or town that has a population over 20,000 determined through the U.S. Census. If the project location meets these criteria at the time of the EB-5 investment then it can be designated as a TEA.

## What is a High Unemployment Area?

In order for an EB-5 project to be considered in a high unemployment area, the rate of unemployment must be at least 150 percent of the U.S. National average in order to get TEA designation. The unemployment area must also be in a metropolitan or county statistical location that has a population of at least 20,000 or more. If an EB-5 investment is made in an area to meets these criteria then it can achieve TEA designation as a high unemployment area.

## How to Get TEA Designation

Get designated as a TEA is a part of the I-526 application. The EB-5 visa applicant needs to provide adequate evidence that their project is located in a place that meets the criteria for either a rural or high unemployment area by providing a TEA designation letter to the USCIS. There are several forms of evidence that can be used in order to prove that the EB-5 investment is being done within a TEA designated area. In order to get this evidence there are several things you can do:

- Contact the US Bureau of Labor Statistic's Local Area Unemployment Statistics (LAUS) office in order to get published technical bulletins.
- Ask for a letter from the state government body in order to provide evidence of a rural area or a high unemployment area.
- Provide other statistical documentation

However, if an EB-5 investment meets the $1 million threshold then there is no need to get the state involved in the TEA designation process. But if the investment is only $500,000 then the involvement of the state may be necessary, but not always essential. There are two different ways you can get TEA designation.

The first is to get designation through USCIS. This requires the applicant to submit evidence from the examples above to prove that the location of the new commercial enterprise meets either the criteria for rural or high unemployment areas.

The second option is to get designation by the state government. An applicant can choose to send a letter from an authorized state government body declaring the location of a new commercial enterprise to be designated as a rural or high unemployment area.

# Step-3: EB-5 Project Investment Capital and I-526 Petition

Once you have chosen a project to invest in and assured it meets the necessary job requirements, and then you need to focus on the required capital investment amount in the project you have chosen. The investment needs to be either $1 million or $500,000, if located within a TEA designated area as discussed earlier. Often the investments are made into an escrow account. After this, an immigration attorney will be able to provide proof of the investment through the filing of an I-526 petition. The USCIS will typically make a decision as to whether or not the I-526 petition is accepted within twelve to eighteen months. Most regional centers will refund the investment amount if the I-526 is denied.

## What is EB-5 Capital?

EB-5 capital is uniquely different from traditional funding sources. The focus of the EB-5 program since its creation in 1990 was to encourage foreigners to invest in the United States and increase American jobs in exchange for a green card. In the wake of the recession and credit crisis, many credit markets have tightened the requirements; making it more difficult for American businesses and developers to get the funding sources they require for projects. As a result, more businesses and developers are turning to the EB-5 program and its funds in order to get the necessary capital for their projects. How does EB-5 program capital benefit the developer? Let's take a look.

## Back Story of the EB-5 Program

As stated before, the EB-5 program was created by Congress under the Immigrant Investor Program for the purpose of stimulating the US economy. Through this program a foreign investor must invest either $500,000 or $1 million, depending on the location of the project as discussed earlier. The project must also create at least ten US jobs.

The program was expanded by Congress in 1992 with the creation of the Immigrant Investor Pilot Program. This is when the EB-5 regional centers were established. Through a regional center, investment funds can be pooled together in a USCIS designated enterprise and allow investors to invest their money in projects that require a larger in flow of capital. However, there is also a benefit to the investor when going through a regional center. This biggest benefit as I've said before is that regional centers allow investors to count indirect and induced jobs toward the job creation requirement. Since an investor doesn't have to worry about creating ten direct jobs per project, multiple EB-5 investors can place their investment in a single project while meeting the job creation requirements in order to get an EB-5 visa and green card.

Consider an example: If a hotel project requires $50 million capital and is expected to create 80 direct jobs and 300 indirect or induced jobs; only eight EB-5 investors could invest either $1 million or $500,000 if only direct jobs were counted as it would be through direct investment. However, this would only raise a maximum capital of $4-8 million of foreign investor funds. If investing is done through a regional center, then the project could count the additional 300 indirect and induced jobs, bringing the total job creation count to 380. This would also increase the maximum number of EB-5 investors to 38, allowing the project to get $19-38 million in foreign investor capital.

While the regional center program is often viewed as a win-win situation, it isn't without its difficulties. Therefore, it is important to consider all the requirements and costs involved while considering all available options.

Regional Center Designation

One way to get the necessary EB-5 capital is for a developer to seek regional center designation from the

USCIS. This process requires the submission of an I-924 application for designation as a regional center and supplemental information that outlines the geographic and industrial area that the regional center will cover, as well as the economic impact and job creation prospects for the proposed projects. The approval process is lengthy and may require responding to multiple requests for evidence, sometimes turning it into a year or more long process.

### Affiliate with an Existing Regional Center

If you are developer looking to get necessary funds in the immediate future, then it may be a good idea to work with an existing regional center designated by the USCIS. Most regional centers will accept new projects from outside developers.

### Direct Investment

Perhaps you are considering the direct investment route. With this option you would be receiving the investment directly from a foreign investor or investors and would not go through a regional center. The benefit of this option is that you wouldn't have to file an I-924 application with the USCIS, but you do have to take into account the fact that there are stricter job requirements with this option, as we discussed earlier.

## Choosing an Investment Method

While the regional center option may seem like the less burdensome option in many ways, it isn't appealing to all EB-5 investors. If you want to start your own business or expand a pre-existing one, or if you simply want more control over your investment and company operations, then you will likely get better results with the direct investment option. Sometimes the option to get permanent residency through direct investment may only be incidental to a foreign investor's primary objective of expanding their business operations to the United States.

In addition, since business ventures will have a higher chance of success in certain regions with better economic conditions, investors who want to maximize their profits may find more options when they choose the direct investment option rather than going through a regional center since most of the regional centers in the United States are located in TEA regions.

Also there is the matter of easier evidence collection when you have greater business control so you can prove you satisfy the legal requirements. With a regional center this evidence burden is slightly less than that of direct investment. Having a strong business motivation isn't necessarily the only reason to choose the direct investment option, since you do need to consider other factors. The most important factor to consider is the feasibility of creating actual, identifiable full time jobs within the business itself for at least ten qualified employees.

On the other hand, the indirectness of the regional center option may appeal to investors who are not as business driven. Regional center investors can use an established, government approved economic unit rather than taking the time and energy to build their own business. In addition to a lighter evidence burden, regional center investors who gain permanent residency will also have more geographic freedom within and outside the United States since they aren't tied to the location where their business is located as are direct investors who are directly involved with their company.

However, choosing to go through a regional center doesn't completely do away with the need for due diligence. If you are interested in investing through a regional center you still want to consider the qualifications of all the available regional centers and their affiliated businesses, including information about government approval, investment experience, success in job creation, financial outlook and visa petition approval rates. All of this was discussed in detail earlier and we will discuss due diligence towards the end.

## What to Keep in Mind

If you are a foreign investor considering the EB-5 visa program then you should consider consulting with an immigration attorney to determine the best investment method for your individual circumstances. An immigration attorney will ask the necessary questions about issues such as those discussed previously in this book so that the relevant features of your individual situation can be considered when deciding the best investment method and the suitability of the EB-5 visa program in general.

Overall, the EB-5 Immigrant Investor Program is a viable and popular option for both developers and investors in a wide range of industries. At the end of 2012 the number of individual immigrant investor petitions or Form I-526 reached an all-time high and 2013 went even higher. When managed properly, individual developers can use it as a legitimate and unique option for financing a commercial enterprise. When used for the right project the EB-5 visa program is excellent for the US economic situation.

## Step-4: Two Year Conditional Permanent Residency

The fourth step in the process of applying for an EB-5 visa is to become a two year conditional resident of the United States so the project funded by the EB-5 investment can be implemented. Once the I-526 petition is approved by the USCIS then the EB-5 foreign investor is eligible to become a US resident. Residency can be attained in one of two ways:

First, if the EB-5 foreign investor has lawful status within the United States already then the investor needs to file a Form I-485 in order to change their status to that of conditional permanent resident.

Second, if the investor doesn't already have lawful status in the United States then they need to apply for an immigrant visa through the submission of a Form DS-230. This form is submitted to the National Visa Center and it must be processed through the US consulate or embassy in the investor's home country.

Both of these options typically require the assistance of an immigration attorney. On average, it takes six to twelve months for an immigrant visa to be issued. During the conditional two year residency period, an investor is required to fulfill the physical present requirements and cannot stay outside the boundaries of the United States for more than a year without applying for a re-entry permit.

## An I-485 Application

After an I-526 petition is approved, an immigrant investor can adjust their status to become a US conditional permanent resident if they are already lawfully within the United States. In order for this to happen, the principle applicant and each of their dependents need to file an I-485 petition. This form is only available to EB-5 investors that are already residing in the United States. If a foreign investor is still living in their home country then they will need to file a DS-230 through the local US embassy or consulate. We will look further at this form shortly.

Form I-485 is the Application to Register Permanent Residence or Adjust Status. Each applicant is required to disclose biographical information to the USCIS with this form so they can determine whether the applicant is eligible for permanent residency. Form I-485 is often filed by an immigration attorney on the behalf of the applicant.

## Components of the I-485 Application

EB-5 applicants must meet several requirements in order to have Form I-485 accepted by the USCIS. The following are the necessary requirements and if you need assistance you should speak with an immigration attorney.

The applicant's criminal history has to be disclosed through the following documents:
- Official statements from law enforcement agents
- Court orders
- Probation records

All valid birth certificates, marriage certificates and divorce certificates. A copy of a foreign birth certificate is required along with copies of all other suitable records.

A photocopy of the complete passport is required along with all immigration related documents proving the maintenance of US immigrant status.

The applicant needs to provide up-to-date photos of themselves. It has to be two identical color photographs that were taken within the last thirty days.

If the applicants are between the ages of 14 and 79 then

biometric services are required. The USCIS will notify applicants of where they can obtain biometric services after Form I-485 has been submitted. Biometric services include fingerprinting and sometimes a photograph and signature.

Applicants must provide a medical examination report along with vaccination records.

For applicants between the ages of 14 and 79 years of age, a Form G-325A must be completed and submitted to provide biographic information. The data collected from this form provides the US government with information to check the petitioner's background. If you can't remember or are unable to find exact dates for some of the information you can choose to put "unknown", but if you do this too often then the USCIS may return the application.

When the I-526 petition is approved then the EB-5 applicant will receive a Form I-797C and a copy of this needs to be included with the I-485 application.

Filing the I-485

As stated before, the I-485 application is often filed by an immigration attorney on behalf of the applicant in an EB-5 program. The I-485 application can be filed once the I-526 petition is accepted since there is no backlog in the EB-5 visa program. The I-485 has an application fee of $985 plus an $85 fee for the biometrics requirement. If the applicant is over the age of 79 then the biometrics fee is waived. Depending on where the EB-5 applicant currently lives, the application is mailed to the USCIS lockbox facility in either Arizona or Texas.

It typically takes six to twelve months for the I-485 application to be processed. The USCIS will notify applicants by either physical mail or email after the application has been processed. While the I-485 application is being processed an EB-5 applicant can obtain work and travel authorization by filing an I-765 application for Employment Authorization and an I-131 Application for Travel Document. Once the I-485 application is approved the EB-5 foreign investor and their dependents will get a two year conditional permanent residency.

Two years after the applicant becomes a conditional permanent resident, then an I-829 petition can be filed to remove conditions and the EB-5 investor will be able to become a permanent full resident in the United States. This also applies to the spouse or any unmarried children under the age of 21 who wants to permanently live and work in the United States along with the foreign investor.

## What is DS-230 Application

If an EB-5 visa applicant isn't already living within the United States, then they will have to file a DS-230 after approval of their I-526 Immigrant Petition by Alien Entrepreneur in order to get conditional permanent residency status during the fourth step of the EB-5 visa process. If an EB-5 investor is already residing in the United States than they can file a Form I-485 as we have discussed above.

The EB-5 investor can file the DS-230 at a US consulate or embassy in their home country for processing. After the form is approved, the EB-5 investor will be given conditional permanent residency status, which enables them and their dependents to move to the United States. An EB-5 investor can choose to hire an immigration attorney to help with this process.

The DS-230 application requires visa applicants to provide biographical information. The applicant themselves will complete and submit the first part of the application, but the second part of the application is filled out and completed in the presence of a consular officer at a US consulate or embassy. The first part of the DS-230 application will collect all the standard biographical information. The applicant will be required to provide a list of previous residences, job history for the last ten years and military service information.

The second part of the DS-230 application is done during an interview at the US consulate or embassy. This part of the application is completed with the help of a consular worker. During the interview an applicant may be required to bring documentation including but not limited to the following:
- Long form birth certificates
- Marriage certificates
- Passports

After the interview is completed, the application is signed. Each family member needs to file their own DS-230 application if they are going to accompany the EB-5 investor to the United States to become a permanent resident.

# Step-5: Unconditional Permanent Residency and I-829 Petition

The final step in the EB-5 visa application process is for the foreign investor and their family to become unconditional permanent residents by removing their conditional two year status. Again the I-829 petition needs to be submitted to the USCIS, but it needs to be done 90 days before the anniversary date that the applicant received their conditional residency.

The I-829 petition proves that the foreign investor has met all the necessary requirements of the EB-5 visa program. It typically takes the USCIS six to eight months to issues a permanent green card after the I-829 petition has been submitted. After this the investor, their spouse and their unmarried children under the age of 21 can permanently live and work in the United States. Then after a five year period from the initial conditional residency, everyone can have the option to become a US citizen.

I-829 Petition

The I-829 petition is the last step in the process of an EB-5 visa for immigrant investors who want to become permanent lawful residents of the United States. The I-829 petition requires evidence that the immigrant investor has successfully met all the requirements of the USCIS EB-5 program.

After the I-829 is approved, the investor's conditional residency restriction is removed so that that investor and their dependents can live permanently in the United States. 90 days before the end of their two year conditional permanent status period ends, the EB-5 investor can file an I-829 petition with the USCIS. While the I-829 is processed, the applicant's conditional residency is extended. The I-829 application needs to be filed within 21 to 24 months of the investor's two year conditional residency period; otherwise the ability to get a permanent residency status can be jeopardized.

I-829 Requirements

An EB-5 investor needs to provide several pieces of evidence along with the I-829 petition in order to prove that they have completed all of the EB-5 program requirements.

A photocopy must be provided of the investor's permanent resident card and the permanent resident cards of all EB-5 family members.

Federal tax returns are required to prove that a commercial

enterprise has been established.

Proof that the capital investment was made in the correct amount is required and can be done through a few options:
- Audited financial statements
- Bank statements
- Evidence to demonstrate that the new commercial enterprise received the investment funds

Proof must be provided that the commercial enterprise has been sustained throughout the two year conditional residency period. This can be done through the following documents:
- Invoices
- Receipts
- Bank statements
- Contracts
- Business licenses
- Federal tax returns
- State tax returns
- Quarterly tax statements

Evidence is required to show the adequate number of jobs were created by the EB-5 project and that the business plan was followed. This is done through two options:
- Payroll records

- Relevant tax documents

All applicants must attend USCIS biometrics by appointment for fingerprints, signature and photograph.

If the applicant has a criminal history then legal documents need to be provided including:
- Law enforcement statements
- Arrest records
- Sentencing records
- Probation or parole records
- All court records relating to the criminal history

## Filing the I-829

An immigration attorney who handles EB-5 matters will typically prepare and file the I-829 application. The I-829 application is submitted through the USCIS California Service Center with a filing fee of $3,750 and a biometric fee of $85. It typically takes six months for an I-829 application to be processed. After the application is processed, an in-office interview with the USCIS or other information may be requested.

## EB-5 Service Providers

As you can tell from this book, the process of entering in to an EB-5 investment and visa program is a complicated and confusing process that often involves interaction with multiple government agencies in both the United States as well as the investor's home country. The paperwork and documentation necessary have to be successfully submitted and this can be a daunting task. All EB-5 investors need to complete and submit petition paperwork along with accompanying documentation such as business plan and various reports. Whether you simply don't have the time and energy to do this all yourself or you simply want to make the process easier on yourself then you may want to consider hiring industry professionals to help make the process quicker and simpler so it is done right the first time. Let's take a look at some of these professional resources that can help you put together the pieces of your EB-5 petition.

### Legal Counsel

Perhaps the most important professional to consider hiring is the immigration legal counsel. Having an experienced and competent immigration legal counsel is something I can't overemphasize. An immigration counsel can provide the central building block that facilitates and arranges all

EB-5 related resource providers. If you are going to hire a legal counsel you should look for an immigration attorney who has specific and documented experience in the EB-5 program process.

The American Immigration Lawyers Association (AILA) is a national association made up of over 12,000 attorneys and law professors who both practice and teach immigration law. You can contact them for a directory of immigration attorneys who are experienced in the EB-5 program process.

An immigration attorney can provide you counseling on all aspects of the I-526 petition process, preparation of all petition and related documentation, representation before the USCIS, liaison services and other resources and all other legal support for the petitions you must file.

Business Plan Preparation

Another critical part to the success of an EB-5 petition is to have the experience of an EB-5 business plan preparation firm. The USCIS requires an EB-5 investor to prepare and submit a comprehensive and compliant business plan that both adequately and professionally describes the proposed business project and required investment. When a compliant business plan isn't submitted then the I-526 petition will likely be denied.

An EB-5 business plan needs to comply with USCIS requirements that were established in 1998 in a precedent setting case known as the Matter of Ho. The case created a list of mandated elements that need to be present in an EB-5 business plan. The list basically clarifies what the petitioner must show in order to establish that the proposed business and the business plan are credible.

The list of required elements including the following:

- Budget and financial projections
- Personnel experience
- Description of the business
- Marketing plan with target market analysis
- Business structure
- Staffing timetable for hiring
- Required licenses and permits
- Job descriptions
- Competitive analysis

A lot of these required elements are challenging and complicated to figure out and put into writing. In addition, they have to be presented with extensive detail and professionalism. The best way to make sure your business plan is prepared according to the mandate of the USCIS is to hire a professional from an EB-5 business plan writing company.

Basically, the business plan needs to show how a proposed business will utilize the EB-5 investment in order to stimulate the economy and create jobs. When you hire a professional business plan preparation firm then you can have the confidence that the business plan has the best possible chance of getting approved by the USCIS. A professional business plan company will know the requirements of the USCIS and will also know how best to show that the requirements are likely to be filled by the foreign investor filing an EB-5 petition.

The more detail your business plan includes with your EB-5 petition, the better your chances of getting success from a reviewing agency. The reviewing agency needs to be able to draw "reasonable inferences" about your business' potential viability from your business plan. Along with assistance from an immigration attorney, a professional business plan preparation can be an important outside resource for those looking to get their EB-5 visa.

## Economists

As noted earlier, Matter of HO requires an EB-5 foreign investor to document both job creation and economic impact from their EB-5 investment within their business plan. While there are a variety of ways in which this requirement can be shown, the best way to meet this important requirement is to provide an economic study that is prepared by a professional economist. A professional economist knows the economic language that the USCIS examiners want to see when it comes to the proposed project's economic impacts. An experienced economist can make a convincing argument for your project through statistics and charts, but more so they can back it up by solid calculations and assumptions. When you can prove that an EB-5 project will create the required ten full time jobs and that the anticipated economic impact justifies the project, it will be easier to get approved of the I-526 petition.

The best way to find a qualified economic consultant is to check with the National Association for Business Economics (NABE). This is the largest international association of applied economists, strategists, academics and policy makers who are focused on the application of economics. The association divides their membership into various subject oriented subdivisions known as round tables. This makes it easy for you to find an economist who is experienced in the type of business you are proposing through your EB-5 petition. Sometimes a business plan firm will also offer this service through an experienced economist that they use regularly.

## Marketing Company

It is also important to consider the services of an experienced marketing firm that has represented similar businesses in the same industry as the proposed EB-5 business. A marketing firm can help conduct a market study and to prepare a competitive analysis, both of which can help a foreign investor to prepare the necessary marketing plan. The EB-5 business plan also has key requisite elements. The USCIS will often want to see that the proposed business and its investor has done a serious analysis of the marketplace and has a solid plan in place to market and differentiate the proposed business. Marketing is also a very important element in having a successful business. Again, some business plan preparation firms have good resources that can either directly prepare a market study or can connect you with an experienced marketing firm in order to help you fulfill this requirement.

If you want to be successful in your EB-5 investment then

you should make use of all available professional resources. While using professional resources can cost more, this expense is often offset by the improved success rate that is seen by those who have a strong and professional business plan. It will make all of your petitions and additional documents easier to submit to the USCIS.

## Due Diligence

As I stated earlier, I wanted to get into due diligence again. When you take the time to do due diligence you can be sure you are getting a sound investment, but you can also protect your investment and ensure success of your business in the future. So let's take the time to consider how you can do your due diligence in making sure everything is done right.

### What to Ask a Regional Center

There are three main categories for EB-5 projects
1. Regional center based projects
2. Direct EB-5 projects
3. Pooled investment projects

The investment requirements are the same for all three of these types. It can be either $1 million or $500,000 depending on the location. However, the three types are slightly different based on the paths they take. Before you consider an EB-5 investment there are a few things you need to consider.

## Investor Profile and EB-5 Involvement

For the direct EB-5 context, an investor is usually driven by a business focused view. If you fit into one of the four following categories then a direct investment may be a good idea:

1. An interest in starting and/or managing a business
2. Motivation to actively control the investment and a desire to make day-to-day decisions on the business project
3. An interest in residing in the area where the business will be
4. A desire to maximize the profit from an investment

In the regional center or pooled investment paths, an investor typically has a more passive role and little interest in managing a business. With these paths an investor can also choose to invest in a project in one part of the United States, while living in a different part of the United States. These investors often still maintain other businesses outside of the United States and spend a lot of time traveling. Profit maximization is often not a top priority of the investment since the rate of return is often lower than a direct investment path. On the other hand, the regional center path often provides the quickest and most secure exit strategy.

### Timing

The biggest benefit to the direct investment path is that I-526 processing times for a conditional green card are often much faster; around two to six months. This is often due to the fact that the deal structures are typically not as large and complicated as a regional center project. However, when larger developers start exploring direct deals then the processing times may be impacted in the future.

When it comes to a regional center path, the I-526 processing time is about twelve to sixteen months or sometimes longer for the foreign investor. In theory, if the USCIS approves an initial investor within the twelve to sixteen month time frame, then the remaining investors will get faster approval since the USCIS will be focused primarily on the source and path of funds for each subsequent investor. While there is no consistency in larger projects this can be a motivating factor for later foreign investors.

The processing time for a pooled investment path can be somewhere in the middle time frame of a direct investment and regional investment.

## Job Creation

Most large EB-5 projects tend to be structured through a regional center since the job count is often higher. This is because a regional center allows indirect and induced employment to qualify for job creation requirements. This means that rather than each investor having to prove their capital contribution is resulting in the creation of ten full time qualified US worker employees supported by tax documents, EB-5 investors can have it covered by a regional center. You don't get this benefit with direct or pooled paths. A professional EB-5 economist will calculate the job impact that comes from capital contribution. When it comes to greater job number with a regional center project, most developers prefer to choose this path.

## Due Diligence

If an investor decides that the regional center path is preferable, then there two main issues to consider:
1. Due diligence to get your green card
2. Due diligence to get your investment back if the I-526 is denied

While these considerations mostly apply to those with a

regional center path, many also apply to the direct or pooled paths as well. Some questions to conduct during your due diligence include the following:

### Has the Regional Center Actually Been Designated by USCIS?

You can get your answers to this question from several sources:
- The USCIS website
- The directory at EB5Investors.com
- The regional centers website
- An online search for public records
- Advice from an immigration attorney

Of course, just determining that the regional center has approved designation doesn't mean that the USCIS has approved the individual project unless it is an exemplar-approved project. You should also keep in mind that some regional centers participate in soft marketing while the designation is pending. During this time no I-526 petitions can be filed until the regional center is officially approved.

### What is the Regional Center's Track Record?

It is important to research the regional center's success rate for I-526 and if necessary I-829 applications. While past success can't guarantee future success, the track record does provide a valuable insight into the regional center and how likely you are to find success with your investment.

## How Long the Regional Center Been Operational and How Many Projects Has It Sponsored

If a regional center is new this isn't necessarily a bad thing, but rather you want to focus on the expertise of the regional center principals. Keep in mind that there are many pending regional center application submitted by credible and successful project developers throughout the country. Just because a principal is new to EB-5 doesn't mean they are new to project development.

On the other hand, if you are dealing with an older regional center, you want to consider how active the regional center has been. For example, if a regional center was approved in 2009 but hasn't worked on any projects since then an investor will want to determine if the regional center has maintained their regular filing obligations with the USCIS and whether or not the ownership structure has remained the same.

The same focus should be placed on researching the developers in a pooled EB-5 project. Before you invest in a project that is going to be handled by a third party, an investor should do their due diligence on all individuals involved.

## What is the Reputation of the Project Developer?

Remember that your fate as an investor is ultimately in the hands of the developer. Therefore, you should research the development team's experience and background and stay alert for any red flags.

## What is the Reputation and Experience of the Project Developer's outside Counsel and Consultants?

An important point for this experience is that of immigration counsel, securities counsel and economists that are involved in the deal.

## Has the Project Been Pre-Approved by the USCIS?

If you are an investor filing your I-526 months after the first project investment then you should determine whether the project has been pre-approved by the USCIS. If the project is pre-approved then this is a very good and positive thing for you.

## Is the Project Being Developed in a Targeted Employment Area (TEA)?

This is a critical question since the answer will determine if your required investment amount is $1 million or $500,000.

## How Will the EB-5 Funds Be Released to the Project?

You may not think this is an important question, but it has a large impact. If your investment remains in escrow until your I-526 petition is approved then you can have more control over your investment. Most developers, however, are leery of this option since it means the capital investment necessary for the development of their project is not available for twelve to sixteen months or two to twelve months with a direct or pooled investment. As a result of these two views, there are many hybrid release mechanisms to choose from. It is best to take the time to consider which option is best for you.

## How Are Funds Returned to the Investor If I-526 Petition is Denied?

In most cases, the developers will return your full capital investment if your I-526 petition is denied. However, there is an administrative fee of $45,000 to $50,000 on top of your capital investment and in some cases only a portion of none of this is returned. So it is important to consider how much you get back if the petition doesn't progress.

## What is the Exit Strategy?

This is definitely an important question to consider with your due diligence. As an investor, you should realize that there is never a guaranteed return of investment. If there is a guarantee like this in the project documents then it should be a red flag since the investor's contribution needs to remain "at risk" until the I-829 is approved. However, there can be a proposed exit strategy should the project prove successful. For example, it can be sold to a third party or refinanced by other equity. It is highly recommended that you as the investor retain a financial professional to help you do a business risk analysis of the project you are considering.

## What is the Rate of Return?

No one wants to waste money and as an investor it is important to ask what your return on investment will be.

## Is There a Job Cushion?

Remember that as a foreign investor through the EB-5 program you need to create at least ten jobs. The greater the job creation above this number, the more assurances you will have that the job creation requirement is met. However, if the job creation cushion comes from impermissible or complicated job forecasts then it may not be a true job cushion.

### When Will Job Creation Occur?

Since EB-5 program rules require the job creation requirements to be fulfilled within two and half years after I-526 approval this is an important question to have answered. For example, if the project has some type of bridge financing then the deal structure is important in determining the job creation time frame.

### What Type of Investment Is Being Made with the Investor's Funds and How Are Jobs Created?

As a foreign investor it is a good idea to retain immigration counsel to help you with advice on whether or not the job creation methodology is acceptable by the USCIS.

### What Percentage of the Total Capital Stack is Comprised of EB-5 Money?

As an investor you likely prefer a project that has a developer who is making a sizable contribution in the form of either equity or additional financing. Therefore, you should be wary of a project that relies only on EB-5 capital for its funding.

## How Credible is the Business Plan?

One of the basic requirements of the EB-5 program is the business plan that must meet Matter of Ho compliance. You can get advice on this issue through immigration counsel. However, it is important to determine the credibility of the project.

After getting your answers to all these questions it is up to you as the investor to determine how much risk you want to take and whether or not the individual project is a good idea for you.

## Permanent Residency

Once you have finished all of the work involved in the EB-5 program you are ready to get your permanent residency or green card. This immigration status allows you to permanently live and work in the United States. Foreign immigrants who get lawful permanent residency are given a permanent residence card or green card. Permanent residency status is granted to EB-5 visa applicants after their I-525 application has been approved by the USCIS. However, at this point in the EB-5 visa process that permanent status is conditional for two years. This allows the investor to come to the United States in order to oversee their investment for two years. At the end of this conditional period, the investor can apply for full permanent residency through the filing of an I-829 application. After this application is approved then the investor and their dependents can permanently live and work in the United States for the rest of their lives. After five years they are also able to have the option to apply for full US citizenship.

# E-2 Visa A to Z Explained

Also known as treaty investor visa.

The E-2 Investor Visa allows an individual to enter and work in the US based on an investment you will be controlling while inside the United States. This visa must generally be renewed every two years, but there is no limit to how many times one can renew. The investment must be "substantial." Investor visas are available only to treaty countries which include countries like Albania and Senegal, but do not include Brazil, Russia, India and China (BRIC Countries).

In this visa, you can choose to start a new company or business or buy an existing one. The investment must be large enough to start and operate the business. The amount of investment varies based on the type of business. The investment will not be considered substantial if it is not large enough to capitalize the venture. The USCIS will use an 'Inverted Sliding Scale' to figure out whether the investment is substantial in proportion to the overall cost of the business or not.

### E-2 Investor Visa Qualification Requirements

- A person or persons with citizenship of a country having a qualifying investment treaty with the

U.S. must own at least 50% of the shares of the U.S. Company; such person or persons may not have permanent resident status or reside in the U.S. under a visa other than the E-2 visa.

- The investment must be substantial and must be made with personal funds (or with a loan secured by property that belongs to the investor personally). While the regulations do not state a specific minimum investment, the investment must be sufficient to establish a profitable business with development and expansion potential.
- The company must contribute to the local economy to an extent that is more than marginal, i.e., the investor cannot invest solely for the purpose of earning a living. Beyond paying the investor a living salary, the business must employ U.S. workers and produce a profit.
- Applicants must show that they have work experience and credentials that qualify them to perform the job that the company is offering them, and the investor must intend to enter the U.S. solely in order to manage and direct the business.

## Additional E-2 Investor Visa-Related Information

The spouse of an E-2 visa holder may obtain a work authorization to work for any employer in any type of job.

- The business activity of the investment company can be changed or expanded into new fields of business.
- Presently, there is no limit to the number of times an E-2 visa can be renewed, as long as the business continues to qualify.

The E-2 visa is generally applied for at the U.S. consulate in the applicant's country of residence. E-2 visas are issued for the period of time permitted under the treaty with that country. If the applicant is in the U.S. in valid status, he/she may also apply for a change to E-2 status with USCIS, but, the status is lost when the applicant travels outside the U.S., and he/she must re-enter with a visa.

### Benefits of E-2 Visa

1. Less investment amount than EB-5 (Typically $1 million for EB-5, and around $50,000 for E-2 visa)
2. No annual cap or quota on the number visa
3. This visa covers the spouse and all children under 21

4. Can be renewed an unlimited number of times as long as the business is in good running condition
5. Eventually, can apply for permanent residency status

## 10 Most Commonly Asked Questions About E-2 Visa

### Does the business need to be fully operational at the time of filing?

No, the investment does not need to be fully operational in order for you to receive an E-2 investor visa. However, the "active" investment requirement must still be met. This means that the business cannot be purely theoretical when you apply for an E-2 investor visa. If you can show that you are making real substantial progress toward the operational readiness of the business that should suffice in most cases. For example, if you can show that you made a purchase agreement with a seller of a business, you opened up a US business bank account or that you transferred some funds to an escrow account, or that you already filed to incorporate your business in the U.S. will show enough proof that you are actively working towards your business.

## What and How Much should I invest?

The investment must be "substantial", taking into account only those financial transactions which are personally at risk. Typically, this means that you are actively putting up your own money for the operation and setting up of the company. Funds must be from legitimate sources, and the funds need to be irrevocably committed. Meaning once you commit, you can't take the money away from the venture once you receive your visa. The government wants to see that you are fully committed to the business and not actually trying to peruse a visa to stay in the U.S.

## What is considered a "substantial" investment?

The nature of the substantial investment depends on many factors. Most importantly, whether an investment is substantial will depend on how much it costs to operate and run the business. Because the amount of funding to effectively run a business will depend on the nature and type of the business, there is no "Magic number" when you apply for the E-2 investor visa. Typically, your investment should be at least $50,000. (Although there can be exceptions even to this amount).

If your business has a lot of overhead and operational costs, then the amount invested will need to be higher. However, if the business has low overhead costs, then the amount for the investment might need to be less. Most importantly, the dollar amount invested must meet the "substantiality" test.

### What is a "substantiality" test?

According to the "substantiality" test, your investment must be proportional to the total value of the particular business you are investing in/starting, or the investment must be an amount that is typically considered necessary to establish and make your business viable.

For example, say it only costs $100,000 to operate and run your business. In this example, you should probably plan on irrevocably investing 55% of the operational costs, or $55,000 to meet the substantiality test. If your business has operational costs of about $200,000, you should probably invest at least 50%, or $100,000.

### Can I have part of the total business price financed by the seller?

Yes, you can but remember your own investment has to exceed the amount you finance. Say for example the business you are buying cost $100,000, but you made a deal with the seller to put only $40,000 down payment and the seller agreed to finance the rest which is $60,000 against the business. You will most likely not get the visa approved. In this case the loan or financed amount is greater than the amount you are actually investing. Instead, if you make a down payment of say $60,000, then you are only financing $40,000 or 40% of the value so in this case your investment becomes substantial and this way you should qualify for under the E-2 visa guideline.

## Does my investment need to be from Personal source?

Yes, only those investments that you personally risk in the event that the business fails will be counted for the substantiality test. The U.S. government wants to see that you are personally financially tied to the success or failure of your business.

## Does the business need to create jobs?

Initially it is not necessary for your business to create jobs. However, your business plan should indicate that the business will create jobs in the future.

According to the requirements for the E-2 investor visa, your investment cannot be marginal in nature. In other words, your business cannot be created only to support you and your family. Any business or investment that you are interested in creating in the United States with an E-2 investor visa should ultimately create job opportunities as your business becomes more successful.

## What is a "marginal" investment?

In order for the investment to qualify for an E-2 investor visa, your investment must not be marginal. The best way to show that your investment will not be marginal is to have evidence that demonstrates that your business is likely to hire more employees — especially U.S. workers — as it becomes more successful.

An E-2 investor visa may be denied if it appears that the business investment was only created to support you and your family. Remember, this should be a business that you plan to grow, and hiring other employees (other than your family) should be part of your business plan.

Remember you are given this visa so you can contribute to the US. economy and not just for you and your family, but for the local community where you can offer employment to local people.

## What is an "essential" role in the business?

When you apply for E-2 investor visa status, you must play an essential role in the business. In other words, the scope of your employment must be to either develop or direct the investment, or you must be a qualified manager or specially trained and highly qualified employee, whose employment is necessary for the development of the investment.

### Who can have the "essential roles"?

These following people are considered to have the essential role in business:

1. Principle investors
2. Treaty nationals who are serving in a managerial capacity
3. Treaty nationals who serve in technical capacities that require special training and qualifications that either work to establish the company, train or supervise other employees, or continuously monitor and develop product improvement and quality control

Employees other than the original investors must be essential for the operation of the company. Basic employees, such as customer service or custodial positions, generally do not qualify as essential business position.

### List of Countries that have the Treaty for E-2 Visa

Countries that Maintain Treaties of Navigation and Commerce with the United States for E2 Visa Purposes

Albania, Argentina, Armenia, Australia, Austria, Azerbaijan, Bahrain, Bangladesh, Belgium, Bolivia, Bosnia & Herzegovina, Bulgaria, Cameroon, Canada, Chile, China (Taiwan), Colombia, Congo (Brazzaville), Congo

(Kinshasa), Costa Rica, Croatia, Czech Republic, Ecuador, Egypt, Estonia, Ethiopia, Finland, France, Georgia, Germany, Grenada, Honduras, Iran, Ireland, Italy, Jamaica, Japan, Jordan, Kazakhstan, Kyrgyzstan, Latvia, Liberia, Lithuania, Luxembourg, Macedonia, Mexico, Moldova, Mongolia, Morocco, Netherlands, Norway, Oman, Pakistan, Panama, Paraguay, Philippines, Poland, Romania, Senegal, Singapore, Slovak Republic, Slovenia, South Korea, Spain, Sri Lanka, Suriname, Sweden, Switzerland, Thailand, Togo, Trinidad & Tobago, Tunisia, Turkey, Ukraine, United Kingdom and Yugoslavia.

This is the most updated list available at the time of writing this book. For an updated list please check the USCIS website.

## How to Apply For an E-2 Visa

First, you need to find a good immigration attorney who has vast experience in investment visa petition process then you can find a suitable business that fits your budget. Make necessary deals with the seller, or partners, draw up all legal documents through an attorney, transfer funds to an escrow account. Do the closing, start running your business actively and then gather up documents and then apply for the visa. It is usually a good idea to have an independent 3rd party person who can help you avoid disaster, scams and fraud especially since it is a rather large purchase and you don't know the seller or anyone else involved in the transaction.

Make sure to provide above and beyond what is usually asked of you to submit as proof

List of Documents you need to Apply

1. All necessary forms DS-156 and DS 156E (You can get these forms from USCIS website)
2. valid Passport
3. One 2×2 photograph
4. Original I-94 (arrival-departure record)
5. Visa Fee

A detailed letter written on the company's letterhead and signed by the designated officer of the company explaining the nature of the business, how the applicant's investment is spent and what his or her daily duties and responsibilities are:

1. The incorporation of the business in the U.S.
2. The ownership of the company
3. the capitalization of the business
4. the business plan

5. Information on business activities such as marketing documentation, sales contracts, and customer lists, etc.
6. Lease or property ownership documentation
7. Financial statements and tax return for the U.S. business
8. IRS issued Employer Identification number or the EIN number
9. All copies of business licenses
10. Escrow documents
11. Proof of all funds transferred to the US
12. Payroll summaries including employment tax filings
13. Company Bank Statements
14. Company Utility bills
15. Any bill of sale or purchase agreement
16. Valuation of the business assets
17. Any foreign tax returns
18. Foreign bank statements
19. Property ownership documents foreign or US
20. Loan or Mortgage documents US or foreign

## L-1 Visa A to Z Explained

Also known as intra-company transfer, the maximum you are allowed to stay under this visa is 7 years.

L-1 visas are available to employees of an international company with offices in both the United States and abroad. The visa allows such foreign workers to relocate to the corporation's US office after having worked abroad for the company for at least one continuous year within the previous three before admission in the US. The US and non-US employers must be related in one of four ways: parent and subsidiary; branch and headquarters; sister companies owned by a mutual parent; or 'affiliates' owned by the same or people in approximately the same percentages. The L-1 classification also enables a foreign company which does not yet have an affiliated U.S. office to send an employee to the United States to help establish one, with additional requirements

So as you can see L-1 is not for everyone, but keep in mind most L-1A visa holders can apply for green card in EB-1C category and do not have to file for any labor certification like most H-1B applicants, not to mention the green card can be approved in less than a year in most cases.

## L-1 Visa requirements

- The company must have a relationship which makes them eligible for this type of visa, such as an affiliate company, another branch or subsidiary in another foreign country.
- The company must also be, or will be, doing business as an employer in the United States and in at least one other country directly or through a qualifying organization for the duration of the beneficiary's stay in the United States as an L-1. This does not mean though that this organization is doing international trade. Doing business in those terms mean positioning goods/services regularly in other foreign countries

## Benefits of L-1 Visa

The L-1 visa is not country specific, and it is a "Dual Intent" visa. Dual Intent means that applicants are not required to maintain a foreign residence and may apply for a green card later, which is a fast track process compared to any H-1 visa to Green card process, as it does not require any labor certification from the department of Labor.

## Types of L-1 Visa

There are two types of L-1 visa

- L-1A Visa, this visa is for managers and executives of a company
- L-1B Visa, this visa is only for the special skilled workers for the same company

**L-1A Visa Requirements**

- The employee must have worked abroad for the overseas company for a continuous period of one year during the preceding three years before entering the U.S..
- The employee must have been employed abroad in an executive or managerial position, also known as a qualifying position.
- The employee must be coming to the U.S. Company to work in an executive or managerial position. According to federal law, executive capacity generally refers to the employee's ability to make decisions of wide latitude without much oversight.
- The employee must be qualified for the position by virtue of his or her prior education and experience.
- The L-1 visa holder must intend to leave the U.S. upon completion of his or her authorized stay.

## L-1B Visa requirements

- The employee must have worked abroad for the overseas company for a continuous period of one year during the preceding three years before entering the United States.
- The employee must be seeking to enter the United States to render services in a specialized knowledge capacity to a branch of the same employer or one of its qualifying organizations.
- Specialized knowledge is beyond the ordinary and not commonplace within the industry or the petition organization. In other words, the employee must be more than simply skilled or familiar with the employer's interests.
- The L-1 visa holder must intend to depart the United States upon completion of his or her authorized stay.
- Following the 2004 Visa Reform Act, an L-1B non-immigrant will be in violation of status if they are stationed primarily at the worksite of an employer other than the petitioner, and if one of the following occurs:
- The alien will be principally under the control and supervision of the unaffiliated employer, or
- The placement at the non-affiliated worksite is "essentially an arrangement to provide labor for hire for the unaffiliated employer," rather than placement in connection with the provision of a product or service for which specialized knowledge specific to the petitioning employer is necessary.

## Documents Required For L-1 Visa Application

### From the U.S. Company

- Article of incorporation or association
- Application for EIN (Form SS-4)
- Stock certificates
- Lease of business location
- Bank statement or wire transfer evidencing initial investment
- Audited accounting reports (balance sheets, profit/loss statements, cash flow reports)
- Corporate income tax return Form 1120 (if any)
- Employer's Quarterly Report Form 941 (if any)
- Description of company business
- Commercial contracts, invoices, bills of lading, letters of credit, etc.
- Bank statements
- Company letterhead (several sheets)
- Company structure, plan of employing new employees
- Pictures of the main office (interior and exterior)

### From The Foreign Company

- Business license
- Article of incorporation
- Income tax filings for the past three years
- Audited accounting reports (balance sheets, profit/loss statements, cash flow reports)

- Organizational chart, total number of employees, position held by the transferee
- Company brochure or product introduction
- Documents of business transactions (contracts, bills of lading, letters of credit)
- Bank statements, or transactional records
- Company letterhead with company logo, name, and address (several sheets)
- Pictures of company's main office, factories, or buildings (Disregard if already included in company brochure)

From the Actual Applicant

- Resume
- Diploma/certificates
- Employment verification letter from the foreign company
- Board resolution or appointment documents verifying the transfer
- Any other documents showing transferee's capability to conduct business in the executive position.

How to Convert L-1 Visa to Green Card

Even though the L-1 visa is a temporary, employment based non-immigrant visa, it is also a "dual intent" visa, meaning that an L-1 visa holder and their dependents may apply for permanent residency without jeopardizing their L visa status.

A specific employment-based immigrant preference category (EB-1C) was created for managers and executives who meet the L-1 standards and are interested in becoming lawful permanent residents. So remember the L-1 to Green card pathway is only for the L-1A type petitioners and not for the L-1B. Having said that, the L-1B can also get a green card but it requires them to go through a labor certification approved from the U.S. Department of Labor

The EB-1 category, or first preference immigration petition, is an employment-based petition for permanent residence reserved for those who are among the most accomplished in their respective fields within the arts, sciences, education, business, or sports. The first preference category is allotted 40,000 annual visas

EB-1C Procedure

1. The employer files Form I-140, petition for an Alien Worker with USCIS.
2. Upon approval of the I-140, the alien beneficiary files for Adjustment of Status, Form I-485, if they are already in the U.S.

# Which Visa is More Suitable For Small Retail Business Like a Gas Station Business

Depending on your funds, you can either apply for EB-5 or E-2. As I just mentioned, EB-5 requires a large capital investment, but the benefit is that you arrive with an immigrant status and get your conditional 2 year green card as soon as you arrive in the US, and that includes all your family members. But with E-2 visa, it is a visa, not a green card, so you are allowed to work and live with your family. But, as I said, not everyone has access to a large sum of funds, so if that applies to you, you may need to take a closer look at the E-2 visa as the investment amount is much smaller. The L-1 visa is the only visa that is not suitable for these kinds of business investment visa because L-1 visa is not an investment visa, it is more like an employment visa.

7 Most Popular businesses to Invest In

1. Gas Station Business
2. Convenience store business
3. Hotel/Motel
4. Franchise fast food restaurant
5. Non franchise restaurant
6. Dry cleaners/Laundromats

7. Mail/shipping business

## Do These Visas Help You to Get Permanent Residency in The U.S.?

With EB-5 visa, there is no delay. As I mentioned you arrive with a residency visa and as soon as you arrive, you get your residency card, this is by far the fastest way to get the Green card, but it also requires the biggest investments. If you are interested in this category, it is best to find out what geographic location offers the least amount of investment. Typically rural areas and smaller cities and States will require the least investment capital, but it is worth checking into.

With E-2 visa, even though as long your business is profitable and operation you can continue to stay in the US and keep renewing your visa, but there is not a clear straight path to a green card for the most part. Now say your business has grown, and now you are employing 10 or more people in your business then you can convert your visa from EB-5 status and thus turn that into a green card easily. For this to happen there is a form I-508 that you have to fill out and submit. You can always apply for a family based green card petition at any time while you are under E-2 visa in the event you have a family member that can file a petition for you.

You should also be aware of the concept of "dual intent" in E-2 status, like other employment-based nonimmigrant

statuses, where you have been allowed to enter the U.S. on a temporary basis. The law requires that, as an E-2 nonimmigrant visa holder, you must return to your country of origin after your work is complete, and you must not intend to stay permanently. However, here is the catch: the law also says that E-2 nonimmigrant visa holders can have **_dual intent_**, meaning that you can simultaneously intend to leave after your E-2 work in the U.S.
complete *and or* intend to seek permanent residence and stay in the United States.

Once you are in business, you can hire an attorney who can then process your application for an adjustment of status where you will be applying for a status change from nonimmigrant visa to an immigrant status.

While under E-2 Visa you can also try to find an employer who is willing to apply for employment-based immigration petition for you and your family. Dual intent doctrine will allow you to remain in the U.S. as an E-2 while your prospective employer goes through the petition process. But be aware that typically employment based immigration is a rather lengthy process as you have to go through and get approved for a labor certification from US Department of Labor.

Here is my take: if you have limited funds and want to move to the US and are willing to work hard in your own business than E-2 is the way to go. Yes it may take a few years to get permanent residency but not having the green card will not affect you in any which way, as you will be allowed to work, travel and do everything else as any US citizen does. Just remember… one step at a time so be patient and follow the rules and things will work out for the best.

## 7 Safety Measures to Protect your Investment

1. First, research and study everything you can find about investment visa process and requirements
2. Find and hire or speak to a qualified and reputable immigration attorney who is experienced in investment visas
3. Contact only licensed local and nationwide business brokers
4. If possible, employ or seek advice from a certified accountant or business consultant who is knowledgeable about your line of business that can analyze sales data and point out discrepancies if there are any.
5. Use an escrow account to transfer funds
6. Carefully analyze sales and financial reports to make sure they will fulfill the visa requirements.
7. Do a thorough due diligence before signing a purchase contract or writing any checks to the seller

## Rights of Permanent Residents

Permanent residents of the United States or green card holders are given many rights. In addition to being able to permanently live and work in the United States, permanent residents can choose to live and work wherever they want unless their direct investment requires them to stay near the business. In addition, permanent residents are fully protected under federal, state and local laws.

Permanent residents can also gain access to one of the best higher education systems in the world and can avoid the international fees charged by colleges and universities. When living in the United States, permanent residents also have access to world-class medical care. Permanent residents are also allowed to travel outside of the United States. While not a requirement of permanent residency, these individuals do have the option to become US citizens after five years.

## Responsibilities of Permanent Residents

While being a permanent resident gets you expanded rights, there are also many responsibilities that you need to fulfill. Perhaps the biggest is that you have to pay all applicable taxes just as any US citizen does. This means that as a permanent resident you need to file income tax returns with the US Internal Revenue Service (IRS). The taxation will be based on the resident's gross worldwide income.

However, foreign investors who come from countries that have a tax treaty with the United States will be able to get credit for paying foreign taxes. Green card holders also need to pay state taxes for the state they reside in while living in the United States. As with US citizens, a male permanent resident between the ages of 18 and 25 has to register with Selective Service. This makes the men eligible to be drafted into the US military in the event that the United States goes to war. Permanent residents also need to remain of good moral character.

## Permanent Residency vs. Citizenship

It is important to note that permanent residency and US citizenship aren't the same thing. A permanent resident isn't allowed to have a US passport. Rather, a permanent resident will remain a national in their home country of citizenship. US permanent residents won't be allowed to vote in US elections or run for political office.

Citizens have an easier time getting their family members into the United States and have better access to federal jobs. US citizens also get more forms of federal assistance and benefits such as Medicare and Social Security.

Permanent residents are subject to physical residence requirements that US citizens are not. For example, a permanent resident may lose their residency status if they leave the United States for over a year without obtaining the proper re-entry permit. Even if they get the proper re-entry permit, they must get a returning visa within two years of returning. They will also lose their residency status if they move to another country with the intention of permanently living there or if they fail to file federal tax returns while living overseas for an extended period of time.

If you want the full rights of a US citizen, then a permanent resident needs to file for US citizenship through the USCIS. You can choose to apply for full citizenship status after being a permanent resident for five years.

## Resources

The information I gathered here are mostly from these websites below.

USCIS Website on E-2 Visa

USCIS on EB-5 Visa

Wikipedia on E-2 Visa

Difference Between L-1 and E-2 Visa

Few Immigration Attorneys I found online

http://www.h1base.com/visa/work/compare%20work%20visas/ref/1133

http://www.nolo.com/legal-encyclopedia/eb-5-investor-who-qualifies.html

visalaw.com

http://www.visapro.com/l1-visa/setting-up-a-business-in-usa.asp

**News in the Media**

CNN news about Investment Visa

LA Times news about Chinese investors Maxing out Visa Quota

www.ingramcontent.com/pod-product-compliance
Lightning Source LLC
Chambersburg PA
CBHW070253190526
45169CB00001B/390